T0272457

My Life in Paper

My Life in Paper

ADVENTURES IN EPHEMERA

Beth Kephart

TEMPLE UNIVERSITY PRESS
Philadelphia • Rome • Tokyo

TEMPLE UNIVERSITY PRESS
Philadelphia, Pennsylvania 19122
tupress.temple.edu

Published 2023

Library of Congress Cataloging-in-Publication Data

Names: Kephart, Beth, author.
Title: My life in paper : adventures in ephemera / Beth Kephart.
Description: Philadelphia : Temple University Press, 2023. | Includes bibliographical references. | Summary: "Highly personal and idiosyncratically historical, this book is a memoirist's guide to more than fifty paper objects, including report cards, maps, menus, spreadsheets, broadsides, library cards, prescriptions, tickets, books, dictionaries, file folder, and legal tender—and an invitation to readers whose stories might be a single box or shelf away"— Provided by publisher.
Identifiers: LCCN 2023010729 (print) | LCCN 2023010730 (ebook) | ISBN 9781439923948 (cloth) | ISBN 9781439923955 (paperback) | ISBN 9781439923962 (pdf)
Subjects: LCSH: Kephart, Beth. | Kephart, Beth—Family. | Printed ephemera. | Authors, American—21st century—Biography. | LCGFT: Creative nonfiction.
Classification: LCC PS3611.E695 Z46 2023 (print) | LCC PS3611.E695 (ebook) | DDC 813/.6—dc23/eng/20230606
LC record available at https://lccn.loc.gov/2023010729
LC ebook record available at https://lccn.loc.gov/2023010730

♾ The paper used in this publication meets the requirements of the American National Standard for Information Sciences—Permanence of Paper for Printed Library Materials, ANSI Z39.48–1992

Printed in the United States of America

9 8 7 6 5 4 3 2 1

For Bill, who travels with me,

for Dard Hunter III, who opened the door,

and for my parents, who forever remain—

in paper and in memory

Throughout the centuries, to this very day, people have taken paper for granted. It is regarded as one of the givens of society, as ubiquitous as rain, smog, motherhood, or oleomargarine. Being so obvious, it has long been invisible.

—Jules Heller, *Papermaking* (1978)

Contents

Prelude

She is old, he says, "stripped to the waist." Her teeth are betel-juice black. Her house is thatch. Her neighborhood is a tangled waterway where mosquitoes incubate, torpedo, whine. All these miles he has traveled to see her—within the swollen belly of a British freighter, by way of narrow-gauge railway, afloat a gondola so low-roofed that for hours he sat on a wooden bench like a serif *C*, I imagine, watching the children and snakes and lizards of the canals in a humid hunch. From his home in Ohio to Liverpool to Singapore to Kuala Lumpur to the settlement of Bukit Mertajam to Padang Besar "on the border of Siam" to Bangkok to here, to a place he calls Bangsoom: a man obsessed with a woman obsessed with the art of making paper.

He says *diminutive.* He says she pounds the khoi-tree bark while her two grown daughters and her ancient husband watch. He, meanwhile—her rolled shirt-sleeved guest—snaps photographs and scribbles his notes and speaks through his interpreter. Asks questions. Gives thanks.

Her mallet in one hand, now in the other, now changing grip again. She sits and pounds on the earthen floor between the teakwood posts that lift the thatch above them—her papermaking a long tradition on this site, a family tradition, pounding back, perhaps, two hundred years, although the particulars of that history are lost to her; she is not the family historian. What she is is hands, muscles, bones—the rhythm she makes with the mallet she wields, the way she frees the bark of its tight fibers.

Paper begins with the loosening of fibers.

Sometimes, she stops and cracks a coconut and offers her visitors a drink, which goes down cool in the one-hundred-plus-degree heat.

Sometimes, she wades down to the clotted stream and distributes the macerated mass across long and narrow woven-cloth molds, then pulls the molds from the stream, drains them, and sets them to dry so that later she, or a daughter, can roll a rounded stick across one paper face to make it right to write on. She performs this act, her observer says, in the manner of Ts'ai Lun (presently known as Cai Lun), the Chinese official employed by the Eastern Han court who, throughout much of history, has been credited with inventing the stuff through which our stories get told, our wealth gets spent, our proofs get proven, our lives get certified, our recipes get passed down, then down (our mother's ink blurring, our father's spill of spices still embedded on the hand-lettered page), our love becomes enclosed.

Yours. My Heart. Forever and Always. Most Truly.

Archeological digs in Central Asia have, in fact, produced earlier paper fragments. Cai Lun, however, maintains his place in paper history as an innovation-minded craftsman (his skills also included the making of weapons and tools) who, in 105 C.E., capitalized on the miracle that you can beat the sense out of rinsed fishnets, tree bark, hemp waste, and last-decade wardrobes; mix the stuff with water in some version of a vat; scoop the freed filaments onto a suspended cloth; and leave what is now congealed, luscious, and blank to dry. For hundreds of years, paper—which is not the sedentary wall of a cave, not the thin splice of papyrus, not the misnomer of rice paper, not the inconveniently hairy vellum, not the clattering of wood blocks, not a pith of stone, not a split pole of bamboo—was one of Asia's most essential technologies, a boon to those with something to say, or calculate, or pass on.

And then: history.

Dard Hunter—an Ohio-born descendent of a long line of printers; a former Roycrofter craftsman skilled at graphic design, book design, jewelry design, pottery, and stained glass; an adventurer who will, over the course of his life, travel more than a million miles to track down the secrets and tools and traditions of those who make their paper by hand—is fifty-two years old when he meets Piung Niltongkum in her thatch house by the brown canal and watches her work among the operatic mosquitoes. He will leave her home with evidence, stories, and lasting impressions, and he will write the next book in his series of books, this one called *Papermaking in Southern Siam*, which, now quoting him, "was quarto in size, with 40 pages of text set in Caslon type and 17 photogravure illustrations from photographs taken in the Niltongkum mill, with the temperature hovering around one hundred and twenty degrees." Only 115 copies of this book will be printed on Hunter's own press, "due to [his] strong aversion to the monotony of press-work." A friend will do the binding. Priced at $27.50 a copy, the book will, like all of Hunter's limited-edition books on papermaking, be an instant sellout success.

And then, Hunter will travel again, in search of more paper, more stories.

We are celebrating Christmas at Thanksgiving, in the well of my brother's house. A doormat, space puzzles, bottles of lemon and lavender soaps, a piggy plant stand, happy Christmas napkins have been unwrapped, and now, extracted from my brother's garden and slipped into temporary paper bags, come the overwintering bulbs of an elephant ear plant and round seeds in hardened, anticipatory pods. After that: my parents' wedding album. After that: a book twice wrapped—a volume, my brother says, that had resided, until days ago, on his dining-room shelf.

"This was Mom's," he explains, as I peel away the gift-wrap layer and stop at the white Plasti-Kleer® Just-A-Fold™ book jacket cover directly beneath. "I thought you should have it."

I lift the shiny white plastic sleeve to find the buff book jacket proper: *My Life with Paper: An Autobiography* by Dard Hunter. Published by Knopf in 1958 and featuring not just photographs of the man's vast journeys but tipped-in sheets of handmade paper, the book was rare by the time my mother bought it, from Bartleby's Bookshop in Chevy Chase, Maryland, on August 14, 2000. She was sixty-seven years old. She paid $100 for her prize. She kept it secure inside its Plasti-Kleer jacket. She kept it, I do not need to imagine, pristine as a secret, and so I do not know what she wanted from Dard Hunter, what she thought of the miles that he traveled, whether, in fact, she even read this book or wanted it for a keepsake.

For what sake, this keepsake?

For whose?

My mother died six years after she purchased this book, a death both slow-moving and catastrophic, and I never knew to ask her. I never knew she knew Dard Hunter, and now here I am, not much younger than she was then, a woman increasingly obsessed with the weight, the sense, the rights of paper. How we carry it. How it carries us. How it holds what memory will not hold. How we battle, commemorate, restore, give thanks, bully grudges, release them through paper. How it goes the greater, surprising distance, stands up to the ask of us—laminated paper as Pullman company car wheels, reinforced paper as the fifty feet of a Prussian chimney, curdled-milk-and-egg-whited paper as the stuff of a church structure in a Swedish parish, paper as the tick and the tock of a watch. This last list according to a story that appeared in the *Saturday Evening Post.*

Baby books. Scrapbooks. Paper bags. Paper games. Paper doilies. Paper news. Paper letters. Blueprints. Sewing patterns. Sheet music. Diaries. Postcards. Mortgages. Report cards. Instructions. Résumés. Syllabi. Certificates of birth and certificates of death. Dollar bills and checks and luminaries. File folders. Dictionaries. Entire libraries. The coptic-stitched, the perfect-bound, the stabbed and sewn, the handmade with the garden flowers. The modest, essential, ubiquitous, fragile. The gifts we wrap with the paper made for wrapping.

Our lives with paper.

Our lives.

Remembering

Dear Dard:

Only because my mother ordered you from across state lines and you were sent whispering to her home wearing your jacket, crisp and white, your title, *My Life with Paper*. Only because she buried you among her sacred things. Only because you came to me as a brother's resurrection, and not as a gift she gave, not as a gift she would have intended to give to the daughter from whom she kept her sacred safe. The things she loved. The ways.

Not a single page of you bent. No crease at any corner. Not a pencil quipping marginalia, scoring a line, splattering an asterisk. Not a loosening in the binding where she might have pressed, her right hand keeping her place on the page, for she was left-handed, her dark alphabet leaning and looped.

If she took notes while she read you. If she read you. If you were there with her at the end, when she lay in the glass box of the room where she died on the bed we rented for her dying. Where she remembered in the order of her remembering, something moving beneath the lids of her eyes, maybe a hope she'd had to write you into the book she never finally wrote, maybe the sound, in her ear, of your best sentence. Did she? Am I fabricating? Exaggerating? Demanding? Dard Hunter, Paper Hunter, Hers: Proof of her private interior world, I never will now open. Late December sun soft on her eternally beautiful face. Orchids on the sill. A bible. A gallery of family faces, framed. And the blue morphine. And the inscrutable haze.

Holding her hand, crushing our distance, there, at the end, when our only words were song, and I was the one singing.

I designed her funeral, her memorial, her place on the hill beneath the carillon chimes, her red granite stone, the distribution of her belongings. I mean to say that I did with my father. After she was gone, I chased her. Chased the winter fox, the yellow bird, the stories that her best friend told, and then I stopped running, and she vanished. Over the hill and gone. A woman it seemed I had never known. A story I stopped seeking.

Then, my brother gave her copy of your book to me—*I thought you should have it*—and to you as some kind of oracle I turned.

Now, there are spits of snow, a cracked cold. Now, this is a teaching day in my city. Two hours from now, I will join a dozen young writers in an acoustically challenged room—the ancient windows open to the ventilating weather, our faces slick beneath our masks, our stifled voices boomeranged by hidden microphones—and I will say, quoting Victoria Chang, who was quoting another, **shorter + shorter + denser + denser + louder + louder**, and I will ask what *silence* is so that we might conduct our filibuster, and I will quote Chang again, this time directly: *Writing is not a choice but an act of patience. An act of listening to silence, into silence.*

But now, in this hour, Dard, in the Van Pelt Library on the University of Pennsylvania campus, among millions of stacked and ordered volumes, along miles of metal shelves, behind walls that slide open, swallow whole, I've been searching for you, and I've come up empty. If I want to hold the other books you wrote—*Papermaking in Pioneer America*, *Papermaking: The History and Technique of an Ancient Craft*, *Papermaking by Hand in America*, *Papermaking in Indo-China*—I'll have to make a reservation in the Kislak rare book room. Leave my belongings in a locker. Sit among the hermitically sealed. Wait for a librarian to retrieve each volume and to place it before me like a sacrifice on a pillow, so that I might turn your pages with a gloved hand. Delicately.

I'd rather stand, I'd rather walk, I'd rather drive: North, to East Aurora, New York, where you learned your early trades. West, to Mountain House in Chillicothe, Ohio, where you letterpressed some of those books you wrote on the paper you made with the type you designed, having the paper that you found inside your travels bound in by your bookbinder. South, to Atlanta, where your one hundred thousand paper artifacts—molds, deckles, watermarks, vats, racks—are museum-protected:

> As I look back over the years, my only feeling is that my life has been wasted. In the present world the only things that count are rush and speed and a desire to get to the moon. My work has been totally unspectacular. If I have done anything worthwhile, it is in the establishment of the Paper Museum.

Your words, Dard. In a letter you wrote.

At a table by a sliver of window, I sit. It is COVID-sparse, and my KN95 has cupped a hot cloud to my nose, my lips, my chin. I am a born hyperventilator; I breathe uneasily. Outside, noon, a chimed descendent of "Here Comes the Sun" riffs off a carillon hidden in the Alumni House just down the walk, because there is no bell tower on this campus, just a small box of sound maintained by a donor's in-perpetuity contribution in memory of a daughter. By which I mean that everything now is a little less true than it was when you were living, or perhaps I mean that the manner and means of our authenticity have changed, the ways we hold and keep us, and your life, Dard, your life was hardly wasted.

shorter + shorter +

denser + denser

I close my eyes. I listen. I remember the story I read in the story you wrote in the book my brother gave me. I was turning your pages—the neat, the swift and crisp of paper. It's your best story, Dard, my favorite. It's the twentieth century, becoming. It's you and your brother, Phil, setting out to give America some magic.

Phil's the actual prestidigitator. He's twenty, calls himself the Wizard. He has taught himself hundreds of now-you-see-and-now-you-don't tricks, and he's famous for them, an elegant mind teaser. For $300 a week, sometimes $1,000, he's been booked by lecture bureaus for jaw-dropped crowds in towns across the country. By passenger train, freight train, stagecoaches, you, together, travel—swerving across Ohio, Pennsylvania, Nebraska, the Dakotas, Florida, Kentucky, Virginia, West Virginia so that he might perform and you, two years his junior but larger in size and so much stronger, might serve as his assistant, a job, you assure your readers, "is no sinecure."

What you do, Dard, is hoist, pack, scrub, file, rinse, place into their proper sequence the hundreds of tools of your brother's trade. What you do engages twenty trunks and "several" packing cases and the crates and the cages and the buckets and the pails in which live your unpaid sidekicks. Rabbits, you say. Ducks. Doves. Goldfish. You care for them all, Dard. You keep the whole miracle of magic untarnished and alive, show to show, town to town, squawk to squawk, don't smash the glass, don't crack the mirror, don't kill the fish, don't let the doves fly away through the room's open windows toward the heat of day, except that, once, in an astonishment of awfulness, a pair of doves do, two diamond rings tied to their necks, while the audience watches in horror.

The Wizard isn't well, but you keep going. The Wizard, who is the smart one in the family, the one who could excel at college if only your parents could convince him to go, wants, more than anything, to keep going.

You want what the Wizard wants. You stack his tricks in their order. You keep him company in those empty train stations, 3:00 A.M., half asleep, ears tuned to the incoming freighter, and there, again, in the ruckus of a "leather-hung" coach, you bounce beside him, hold on, fight against the forces that would catapult you from your seat. You are learning wanderlust. You are all the extra hands, the single pair of legs that races to the local repair shop, mid-show, when the Wizard mangles a watch he has borrowed from the audience—a terrible accident that cannot be revealed. You become the Chalk Talker—a young man with sticks of color and a board and yarns to spin while the Wizard, growing more tired and more tired, catches his breath backstage. You are living the Wizard's dream because time is running short for him, because you'll never have another brother, because tuberculosis has come for him, and he will have to cut his touring short, and he will die, despite careful convalescence, at the age of twenty-seven in 1908.

He will leave you.

"We had been closely associated, and I had long depended upon him for guidance," you write in the book my brother gave me. Telling then of how the Wizard, "a student of spiritualism," hoped desperately to find a way for the dead to communicate with the living, or, at least, for these two brothers, best friends, to never lose the sound of each other. You write:

> [W]ith considerable ceremony, we entered into a secret agreement that whichever of us passed away first would make every effort to communicate with the other. Phil drew up an elaborate code involving mystic symbols and devices so that no practicing spiritualist could possibly deceive. After my brother's death, spiritualistic mediums were given every opportunity to act as mediators between us. . . . But in every instance I was disappointed. The secret symbols devised by him for direct communication between us never appeared.

> After nearly fifty years I have given up all thought of after-death communications.

You mastered wood and color and clay and shine and the swifts and angles of each alphabetic letter before you became obsessed with paper, and then, Dard, you saved your brother on the page. Made sure he did not dodge the frame.

If I have done anything spectacular.

There was Phil, there were the girls, both of them strangers. Dying with you, and persisting. The first one hurtling toward you on a horse set afire, when you were eleven, the son of a printer. You were rich with the world and lodged in a house whose long backyard descended, green, toward the Ohio River. She was a red and yellow stria on a cool spring day, a girl engulfed, her cotton dress scorching, her mount galloping down the drive toward the river, the flames higher than her head now, her hair ashed, and you ran for her. Snagging a horse blanket from your barn and racing behind, until your speed caught up with hers.

Here, you must have said. *Here*. The girl now in your reach, in your hands, on the ground as you snuffed the flames, beat them out with your boots, and you would have saved her, Dard, but she had died.

You were her last touch, her final word.

The other girl was walking a road. You were on your way to Tonkin, to the old papermaking regions of Yen Thai and Lang Buoi, and you might have taken the railroad, but you chose a bus driven by a barefooted man instead. Beside you, on your first-class bench, were the bales of fellow passengers and an odoriferous pet monkey, and on the floor was the expectorated juice of the betel nut masticated by those on the benches behind you.

Bouncing along.

The road was ruts. It was a crowd of women wearing black pantaloons, their bodies bent and swayed by the pots and rinds and seeds on their heads, the bus "continu[ing] at breakneck speed past the endless weary cavalcade of humanity." Now, there was rain. Now, the bus began to stop at the shops along the way, and then again speed ahead, past more weary, awkwardly be-hatted travelers who shared that narrow road, until the driver, his eyes on the rain, or on the clock, struck.

Dull, nauseating thud.

You write, for you knew at once. You left your bench, that monkey, the bus, and hurried down the road, pierced the sudden circle of the crowd. She was "an Annamese girl," her feet bare, her dark hair pulled back into a braid ribboned with white silk. She looked at you, and then she died. You lifted her into your arms. Carried her from the road to the grass, slippery with rain. Laid her down into the earth and left her. You walked the road to the waiting bus. Climbed aboard. Shoved aside the monkey.

A million miles you went in search of handmade paper, Dard, and what remains is story. The scenes still intact. The dead still alive. The evidence of love, shock, wish, the language you chose for remembering, and the suggestion that we weigh our living according to reams. That we make the watermark our claim, and the deckle our prerogative, or perhaps the smooth resulting edge of the metal guillotine. That we reconsider the bleached and the pristine, the dried flower petals with which some pages have been made.

Just a sheet of paper.

Just *this* sheet of paper.

Drying in the sun. Left to rain. To fingerprints. To marginalia. To crackle, bend, defacement, the stranger's gaze, the metal teeth of the public shredder. The Psalm 23 that was torn off by a breeze and left to tumble between cemetery stones like an uprooted weed. The will she will refuse to read. The math on the back of the envelope they saved. The card he wrote but never sent, reading his own apology back to himself, years later, years too late. The teacher's notes on the homework paper. The father's scribbled final wish on the bank check.

We are our own ephemera, and you wished to be paper's purist, Dard. *Noble*, you said. *Craft*. You had no use for—in fact, disdained—the paper made by faceless churn and power. You would have been "content" you write, "never to see again one of those long, ponderous, stamina dragon-like machines emitting from its great jaws the streams of paper that are thought necessary to our very existence."

But the "dragon-like machines" persist in this abundantly impure age, and paper abounds in all of its forms, and it is because of you that I have set out on my own strange, fibrous adventure: to find myself in the remains of paper. To find my yearning, new. To find out what paper *means* and what I might *mean*, if I have more time, if I claim it.

The *what ifs*, Dard. The *if onlys*. The dimensions of our lives that will perpetually elude us.

Baby Book

I was not a baby for whom a baby book was made.

Maybe you find one at the end of a table, in a flea-market parking lot, when there is no baby by that name anymore, just a grown-up, or a ghost, staring out from the pages, and you think, Who?, and you think, When?, and you feel the shame and thrill of trespass, and wonder where your own baby book is, or if there ever was one.

Your mother doting on you. Your mother writing your story.

The whole history to the thing: Dime store–bought or homemade. Lavish, treacly, thin. Mass-produced by Just's Food Company, or the Mother's Aid of the Chicago Lying-In Hospital, or the Home Savings Bank of the City of Albany. Illustrated by famous artists, or artists with famous sons. Or just blank pages. Or pages with rules.

Your mother bending to the categories, ruled lines, colons—or writing in the margins. Accidents, gifts, weights, heights, words. Your mother clipping and saving, preserving and amending. Dark hair curls. Footprints. First bib. First sneeze.

You, the chronicle of her making.

If you had mattered, wouldn't you have mattered like this, you think, standing in the flea-market parking lot, the stranger's baby book in your hand? If you had mattered, wouldn't your mother have given your story its best baby book start, the history of you you cannot otherwise claim, the narrative she might have set in motion?

Scrapbook

But the scrapbook.

A big clunker of a thing with hinged wooden covers that look like they had been wrenched from the paneled walls of a hunting lodge. Rough, scalloped edges. A splash of sea-foam green toward the top right corner: an accident with paint? The word *Album* is cursived across the front in a multi-ply wood of contrasting stain, as if this thing could have any other purpose. The cover biffs when opened. The long, wide, thick, black pages sibilate. The slack parts and pieces drop to the floor.

They drop to the floor like auguries.

They sweep it.

Page 2 is where the action is, the opening line: "It all began here | May 4, 1958." My mother's best handwriting, with the sharp tip of a white pencil. The photographs, square and monochrome. My mother and my brother. My mother and my brother. My brother. My brother. And the captions: *Mommy loves me! So much to see! Ahhh!*

Eyes on the exclamation marks. On my mother, young, rubber cementing corners into hopscotch patterns, editing the family until we, as family, fit. Alignments. Juxtapositions. Intensifications. Exaggerations. Gaps. This is my mother's memoir, the curated version of this chapter in her life, when she is twenty-eight years old. My father is at the refinery. She is alone at home, in Ashbourne

Hills, with babies, something rising in the oven. The question becomes: How has she learned to be this kind of wife, putting her investment down on this version of her family, her shine? *It was like this. We were.* She'll have the first word, the only residual first word, pressing us into the thick, dark, deep, black strata of her scrapbook story, leaving her mind behind, her idea of us, her myth and a gift for the man she loves. She does love him. She respects him. There is proof inside a letter.

Folded twice, so that it works as thirds. White, no watermark. Blue ink.

> December 21, 1961
>
> Sweet,
>
> This is something we'll treasure, and, I hope, add to, for it will become more precious as time goes by.
>
> I had fun doing it, and you may not think so, for it's not very evident at times, but I did restrain myself from being too corny. Anyway, those dear faces need no help from me!
>
> Merry Christmas, Flebus.
>
> Lore

My brother and, after a few turned pages, me. Two rows of me looking up, beyond her, toward a sky that only I, in the photographs, can see. *No comment*, she writes with her white-tipped pencil, and then, sharpening her tool across pages, between scenes:

> I'm 3 years old today and I've got my own Humpty Dumpty Cake.

Our Lizzie Babe.

And here's my Fair Lady inviting Jeffie to a tea party.

She's dear.

Too much.

Cowgirl Bethie.

Such fun we have.

I am, already, so many names. I have no words yet with which to contest her. My dark hair is cropped short to tame its curls. My brother is my best companion, he in his bowtie, me in a dress she made. The story is that goodness found us, that goodness *was* us. Good bones, good bodies, good family.

But now, in the amended version of the scrapbook, the extended Chapter 2, a little tremble. The paper folded in thirds again. The handwriting a bit more erratic:

December 24, 1964

I felt it was time for another pictorial episode in the life of us Kepharts. The past few years have had their ups and downs, good and bad, but somehow always bearable because we all had one another. These pictures mainly record just little, unimportant incidents, but mostly those little things, I feel, make us somewhat unique.

I'm thankful most of all for another Christmas all together—and I suppose, very humbly, for our baby. It would be kind of dull without her, wouldn't it?

Love you,

Lore

Bearable. Dull. Humbly. Wouldn't it? A shift in tone and point of view, as if the enterprise of motherhood has been exposed for what it would become to her—an impossibility of factions and alliance, a weariness of choices, whispers, rumors, hurt beneath the surface, hurt as surface. A family of five is not a family of four, and little children are not babies, and the middle child knows that changes to her mother have come, watch the middle child now as the deep, dark pages turn.

The captions thin.

The narrative slips its corners.

It was the Greek poet Simonides of Ceos (in the Roman legend) who held the original key to the memory palace. How (it is said) he could identify the crushed bodies in a banquet hall by recalling precisely where each person had been sitting before a faulty roof fell and reduced the diners to sticky smithereens.

We might store all our memories in such a way, so the memory palace logic goes—assigning each fleeting moment to a particular location in our mind and taking a mental look-about when we are remembering. Here, by the imaginary stair, our father sneezing. There, on the imaginary stoop, our airedale barking.

On the other hand: scrapbooks—"the material manifestations of memory," as they have been called by chroniclers Katherine Ott, Susan Tucker, and Patricia P. Buckler in *The Scrapbook in American Life*. "It is the self that guides the scissors and assembles the scraps," they write, introducing Giorgio Vasari and his assembled images of art, Samuel Pepys and his albums of London ephemera, Thomas Jefferson and his exercised "gathering and framing," and the actual wooden cabinets of curiosities into which some scrapbooks got lodged.

Ephemeral, 1560s, "originally of diseases and lifespans," "like a fever," the etymologists say. A word that grew into itself and blunders through us, until we are making ephemera with our ephemera, gluing our vanishing down, paging through what others left behind, hunting for truth beside, behind the white-tipped stories.

Photograph

That was me before I knew myself to be green-eyed and dissatisfied with every sentence I would not write. In my mother's arms with my father's gaze upon me and my brother in an ear-flap hat, standing his ground.

That was the house with the sandbox backyard and the streamered bikes and the piano my father sometimes played, still smelling of heat and blaze, refinery fires. The sky before us is behind us in the temperate window glass. It is the way my mother holds me that hurts me most, the way my father already sees himself in his first daughter and anticipates her unseasonable need to smack her palm against the yellow sun and to run, self-glorified, to the crusting sea and mourn for gray-backed dolphins.

Last night, it was much too cold to sit outside, and I sat, and the stars seemed upside-down and scolding, and a blizzard, it had been reported, was on its way, but this was before that, and it was cold, and I was wretched again with the beauty I had failed to keep.

What are we to do with them—the square, the rectangle, the shine, the fade, the crease, the tear? They are our ourselves, our perfect strangers, shoved in with the cutlery we never polish, tucked away as bookmarks, secure within the folds of blue-ink letters. They are the trick of the past we have been beaten to. A cause of shock or shame. A wrenching up of the *was* of us, instructions on what might have been.

What if is the third dimension of the photograph.

Blame it on the man with four names—William Henry Fox Talbot—and many talents who, in the 1830s, thought to dress a fine sheet of paper with table salt and silver nitrate before layering something from the garden down—a buckler fern, say—and sacrificing the whole thing to the sun. What had been exposed to light became dark, a negative, an image that could be used repeatedly to tell the story of a moment that had passed. Talbot's "photogenic drawings" evolved. The process was advanced inside the cameras that he built. By the 1840s, he was patenting his calotype—insisting, alongside Louis-Jacques-Mandé Daguerre and others, that we change our way of seeing not just the world but ourselves.

"How charming it would be if it were possible to cause these natural images to imprint themselves durably, and remain fixed upon the paper?" he said. "And why should it not be possible?"

Imagining a world without photographs is imagining the absence of regret. A few fewer grays. Dilutions of blue.

Menu

She could have anything she wanted, and she always chose the same: the toasted fried clam roll, a real steal. She'd get one, or maybe two, alongside a pot of tea, and Dad would get the hamburg steak and tomato, and I might like my own Small Fry, *thank you, please*, or a Jack and Jill, or the Simple Simon special, or the Frankfurt on the toasted roll with its neon stripe of mustard. We knew to be good at the Howard Johnson's, there on our mother's night off, in our space-age booth, with our children-sized menus, our feet not reaching the floor, not even kicking one another, my father saying, *Should we?*, and us saying, *Yes, please, more*, and so the shakes would come—my father's black and white, and mine like his, the cold thick sweet froth going up the straw and past my nose and straight into my head, while my mother leaned in for her sip.

According to Jan Whitaker, printed children's menus first emerged in the 1920s, "often at department stores and other restaurants patronized by women of comfortable means who were out shopping." Howard Johnson's, which dominated the chain-food restaurant scene when I was growing up, was notoriously child-friendly—its menus catering to the tastes and imaginations of children as well as to the mothers who, after weeks of menu planning at home, would gladly slide into the booths and wait for the cooks to take their orders.

Homework

Homework is what you made and someone saved. It is proof of your mind in a previous iteration. What you were good at, how your pencil slanted, how you stayed or could not stay within the lines. You got it right, or you got it wrong. You were the best of or the least among many, a Goody-Two-shoes, a fighter, a punk. It's all right there, on all that paper, in all paper's forms. It follows you from house to house because you cannot let you go.

You box it. You file it. You share it with your son. The older you get, the more you wonder.

September 15, 1967

How I got ready for school

I bought 3 pencils and a school bag and a lunchbox. I wanted to go to school. I got ready for it. I got some crayons but I didn't bring them to school.

October 11, 1967

Why We Talked?

It wasn't very nice for us to talk. I don't know why we talked. We rally should not off talked that loud or talked any. I hard how loud we did talk it was so loud that it hart my ears. Our class is so noisy that it is like being in a class of 100. It is such a noisy class. At reases we are very noisy. I is like a big buch of cowboys and horses. I a grea it is a noisy class it is a very very very noisy class. I hope our class will not be that naisy. Because it does not sound right. I wasn't talk to anyboddy. But I was saying be giut. It wasn't helping or being nice.

October 17, 1967

If a zebra was in front of your house in the morning when you would wake up you might look out of your window and if you had a dog you'd say someone painted my dog. You might tell your mom. And you would say my dog looks like a zebra. She might say hoo painted it. I would say I do not know hoo painted it. But I would still feed it. It wouldn't eat. I would find out that it was a zebra. But to make shore I'd take a look in the basket. Yes my dog is there. I'm shore it is not a zebra. We would take of him that day. He might have a girl friend. She might come the next day. We would let them stay together for another hour. Then we would take them back where they came form. When we would come home we would find that we didn't have grass.

The crisp lined paper and the soft-bound composition books. The empty boxes where the numbers and their symbols went. The checklists of assignments. The A, the B, the C. The construction-paper art. The punch of the staple. The faded brown where the Scotch tape was. This homework that some say Horace Mann forced into nineteenth-century sensibility before the American Child Health Association screed against it (child labor!) before the Cold War again brought its spate of homework advocates before (time moving on) homework would again be debated.

Did it own us? Did we own it?

Diary

The diary was whatever you wanted it to be, every mood you had a mind for, every strikethrough that you fancied. The diary was the confessions you carried with you all day long, then bored you when you sat to write them down. It was the tedium of your dissatisfactions: your hair, that boy, your best friend. *I am so discouraged. Why do I get the reputation of being so sweet? I want to do something exciting.*

Christmas 1973

Dear Diary:

I'm unusually happy!!

I got Mom—plants.

Jeff—pen and pencil.

J.—ring.

Dad—socks.

Uncle Dan—book.

Grandpop—bathtub mat.

It's the rare exultations you find, turning the pages now, that quietly appease you. Your capacity for happy. And while you don't precisely remember the inspiration for that bathtub mat, or the color of that ring, or the argyles on those socks, and while you hope you went past ordinary in pen-and-penciling for your brother, your lost self was glad to give, according to your diary. All these years gone, and still you thrill to the gift. You are who you were, your diary tells you.

Call it a diary—it is less imposing than a journal, which sounds like an end in itself. . . . Everything goes in: grocery lists, things to do (so I can scratch them off), random observations, knitting patterns, recipes, overheard dialogue, everything. A diary isn't sacred. Think of it as the written equivalent of singing in the shower. I don't care what I'm writing and I don't pay any attention to language. Most of what's in there is boring, but it keeps me in the habit. Writing doesn't have to be good, not at first.

—Abigail Thomas, *Thinking about Memoir*

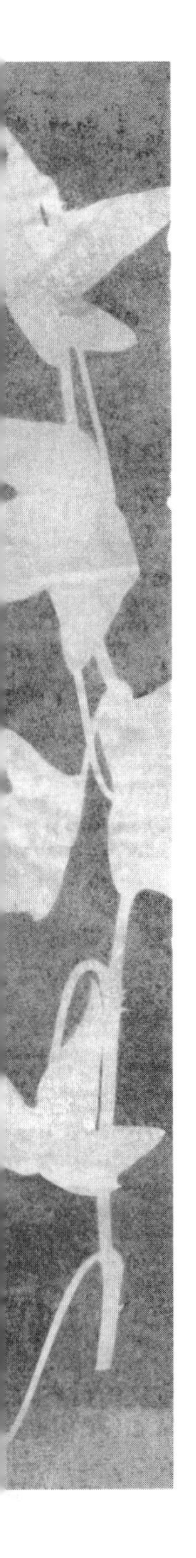

Craft

Dear Dard:

All I was missing was the chalk talker's chalk. My mother, too. She should have been there.

You were every age you ever were. You were the hero of the story. You were six feet and stride, diffident, obsessive. The story of your blanket arms around the burning girl. The story of your hand in Gandhi's. The story of your lonesome days and your partly famous ones. There, in the reading room of the Kislak Center for Special Collections, Rare Books and Manuscripts at the University of Pennsylvania Van Pelt Library, on a bright-sky day, you had been retrieved, which is to say, resurrected, by which I mean we were riotously impromptu in throwing you a party, and I was chalk talking you. My audience was captive.

I was wearing a mask; it was pale blue. I was wearing sneakers; they were stained. I was fogging my glasses with enthusiasm, and yet, when I spoke, they listened. One curator, two curators, three. Bringing me your rare books, Dard, their slight hands your silver platter.

Papermaking in Indochina, published in 1947, number 138 of 182 copies.

Old Papermaking, published in 1923, number 48 of 200 copies.

Primitive Papermaking, published in 1927, number 44 of 200 copies.

Books built to mirror your own dimensions. Big, tall books—close to a foot tall, a full foot tall, five inches more than a full foot tall—and sturdy, never mind the cracking on the spines, the dimples in the morocco leather, the places where the tipped-in art shimmies away from yellowing adhesives, the crooked float of watermarks, the slapdashness of the deckle, the puckering stains along the frontispiece's top edge. I was afraid to touch, to turn. I was aware of the weight of the history there. Of your imagination, and frustration. Of the language you deployed—*primitive*—raising questions you're not here to answer.

My heart was high throb. My attitude was breathless. Look, I said, toward whichever book was, in that moment, resting on its rare-book pillow. Hoping one of the curators with a surer hand would lean down and turn the pages. While I photographed. While I read. You being funny, self-promoting, self-defending. Artifactual, textual, and scrappy.

We are to forgive your books for their misapprehensions, you say.

We are to look upon them as treasure, you imply.

"No out of print book from the Mountain House Press has ever been sold in the antiquarian book market except at a substantial premium above the original selling price," you inform your minor crowd of readers. And: "This book, with all its omissions and errors, is the most comprehensive work on the particular subject as the craft of the old papermakers has received but scant attention."

You will, you say, "make no apologies for the compilation of the text, or for the paper, type, or printing." You own "the many technical faults in the actual making of the book." You hope it's clear that "the entire effort has been a serious attempt at something never before accomplished and the undertaking must be accepted in this light." You are grateful:

> It remains to add a word of explanation concerning the illustrative material in my present book. Whenever possible I have used original specimens of native papers, many of which are exceedingly rare and difficult to procure. When originals were impossible facsimiles from sheets in my collection have been used. These have been made faithful to the originals, and I trust will serve to give an idea of the design, color, and texture, of these primitive papers. The gathering of material has extended over a period of more than ten years and has been made possible by the interest and help of the curators of museums throughout the world, and of many missionaries and correspondents in Mexico, South America, Java, and the islands of the Pacific Ocean.

Your books had been quarantined in the locked-down fifth-floor stacks, but now here they were, in the sixth-floor Kislak sun, in the company of actual rare-book experts, in my temporary possession, and what would my mother say, if she could have seen us all, if she could have been where she should have been, a member of the party? What would she say, I wondered, about the journey that she started, but only accidentally and only long after her passing?

"The layman who has an interest in paper making and printing—and it is an interest easy to acquire and hard to lose—will find it worth his while, however, to examine this book with care if he can come across a copy at some museum or library, or in the hands of some book-loving individual," writes R. L. Duffus, in the *New York Times*, on September 6, 1936, about one of your odd volumes. Continuing:

> He may not realize without being told that the paper comes from the mills visited by the author and is entirely hand-made; that the designs on the board covers are printed from eighteenth-century Korean wood blocks and that the text is set in Monotype Baskerville. He will realize, nevertheless, that type, paper and binding are a pleasure to the eye and

hand, and that the book itself, regardless of what is in it, is a work of art.

That first day with you at the Kislak, Dard, was unequivocal, uncensored. You were oversized and color-saturated, a man I made synonymous with his lore. I wasn't of a mind to challenge my affection. I wanted to be dazzled, and I was.

But now, when I leave my house and board the train, I ride toward you with questions. I deboard at Philadelphia's Thirtieth Street and descend until everything is concourse high. Then, out in the hard knock of city air, I hurry at the crosswalk and turn west, toward Drexel University, then southwest, toward Penn, until I arrive at the Van Pelt library, which has never looked a day more glamorous than its circa-1962 self.

I show proof of my health and proof of my status. The turnstile clicks me in.

I choose the stairs. I climb through the library bowels into the highest distance. Out of breath, sucking at my mask, I stand before the tall windows in the open reading room, arranging my allegiance. Finally, I surrender my worldly things and buzz in to the sacred space. The curators have gone digging. They've found more of you, uncatalogued. They've left stacks for me on their metal cart, artifacts separated by skinny call-number slips.

In this moment, suspended before me on the soft foam cradle, is number 17 of 370 of your *Papermaking by Hand in India*. It is not a book that you built from scratch. It is, instead, the 1939 Pynson Printers edition, printed on Swedish handmade rag, with an ovalized, sepia-toned version of you beside a sepia-toned stranger on the title page. Your height is showing in the photograph. Your vest is wrinkled by heat, your trousers are light in shade and perhaps too long, and you have one hand punched against your side and one hand slipped inside a trouser pocket. You wear a flower lei around your neck—I imagine purple—and your face is solidly constructed, forcibly assertive. There's an entire world between the hard line of your brows and the severity of your hairline, but it's rude to conjecture, and the truth is that I am confused by you, by the tone of you, in the opening lines of the opening pages of number 17. Words hinting at scold. Words connoting judgment. An Othering of those who populate your travels:

> Unless governmental encouragement is forthcoming, which is most unlikely, the handmade paper industry of India will be a thing of the past within ten years. British officials in India do not encourage the making of paper by hand, for every ream so made naturally diminishes the revenue from imported paper. The Indians are hopeless and disheartened; I am wondering if these silent and embittered people would be cheerful and contented if they were suffered to go their own way, free from the political dominance of Great Britain and from alien religious influence.

Hopeless, you write, categorically. *Embittered.* And yet: In Kashmir, Sailkot, Delhi, Agra, Kalpi, Wardha, Hyderabad, and Dacca, you were welcomed and cared for by priests, teachers, merchants, and artisans, by papermakers with tapered fingers and turbans, who, in the heat of their days, mixed, macerated, poured, left paper to dry in the sun. You crouched beside them. You composed them into photographs. You heard, I imagine, their songs. You shared their hours. You carried their yield home to Chillicothe, and into each colorfully clothed quarto volume you had bound twenty-seven multicolored, multitextured, multisized exemplars of what they'd made, in the way they'd grown to make it, with the hands they trusted to your gaze. Your hosts would become who you would allow them to be; they would, forever after, stand on *that* stool, look in *that* way, draw their blankets across their chests against the cold on *that* earth on *that* day.

"Every time you tell a story, the story changes," Radha Pandey will tell me, months from now, when we are talking about you. She is an exquisite book artist, Dard—a woman who gives the books she makes narrative names like *Taking Stock* and *Deep Time*, a woman who once, over the course of a July 4 weekend, stood in your Mountain House home, at your iron handpress, printing postcards on paper you had made, with type you and your son had left behind. Your old press is heavy, Dard, inhumanly heavy. Radha's partner pulled, she pushed, they worked deep into each night, awed to be among your things, to be choosing, setting, inking.

But Radha had also, as a student, read you, she will tell me, considered you, thought about your travels there in India. Your clean housing. Your prepared food. The papermakers you depicted, with your images and words, as unhappy and belabored and *exotic*—as people beaten by work, politics, and sun. *Hopeless. Embittered.* Were there other stories? Other explanations? Other adjectives? Might there have been? There is no altering the history you made, she will remind me. There is no second chance for the delineated. No going back in time and rearranging the gaze.

The livelihoods of the papermakers of India became part of your legacy, Dard. Their work was indivisible from your own. Your book exists because of them, just as this book, Dard, *my* book, is inseparable from you and from every person from my life—fiercely loved and equally confusing—whom I have worried onto its pages, crafted. Material as memory. Remembering as tone. Tone as judgment. Judgment as history. What is ours to have or name? What should we make of our making?

I stand here turning pages, Dard. It's quiet at the Kislak.

Paper Bag

Close your eyes, he says. *Then, hold your hand out flat.*

I do.

Don't open your eyes.

I don't.

He rustles his hand inside the paper bag—the banged-up, bumped-out, flat-bottomed paper bag. He is a man of crumpled, overused, Kraft-made paper bags, driving them all this way, from his house beside the shore.

My mother's brother. The one who loves me best.

He rustles more. He makes me wait. *What do you have?*, he asks, now placing the found, mysterious thing in my upturned hand. I have something weightless, itchy as an old man's untempered eyebrow would feel, were it stretched across my palm.

Now, he says. *Open your eyes. See?*

A stripe of gold running the diagonal of my hand. A pipe cleaner, long-haired and shaggy. We are sitting in the family room, in a trapezoid of sun, and I am holding flutter.

It's the start of a nest, he says, taking it back into his pinch. He wraps the pipe cleaner around his thumb and presses the bottom coils snug, into a bottom. The nest is gold, small, fringy.

Again, he trusts the gold to me. Again, I wait. He dips his hand into another crumply, noisy paper bag and retrieves yellow finches and a pile of silver clips. With Elmer's glue and peeling fingertips, with hard, faceted nails left long enough to tuck, press, and pull, he fits the nest with a finch and clip.

From the saggy well of his paper bags, he pulls supplies. I coil, he bottoms the nest. *Pinch.* The finch lands, he glues, I clip. We leave the clipped birds perched in their fringed nests to dry in air that is sticky, sweet, and now there are more secrets hidden in the bursting paper bags. Paper bunnies and paper Santas and paper Valentine hearts and paper girls peering out at us from the pages of the Victorian scrapbooks he has found and bought at countless flea-market sales. Reels of velveteen. Lace, like cake doilies. False pearls, short pins, elaborate inch-high cardboard cutouts with which he will, with tweezers and a mind for 3-D, build verisimilar scenes.

Bubble worlds, I think.

Dioramas, he explains.

He needs my help. I am best at this. Love is power. Watch us making cards. Big, tall, wide, fancy, every one a spectacular. We cut rectangles of velveteen and glue them. We cut pictures from the scrapbooks, glue them too. We fix gold netting across the scenes we make, *a touch of the mysterious*, he says, even more fancy. Working with precision inside the fumes of glue, on the creak of the card table, in the family room, by the light of the sun. Making our corners straight. Imagining whomever will buy the card and whomever will get the card—runnels of rumor about imaginary people, and nobody knows but us.

Beyond the window is the narrow breezeway, and past that there is the driveway, the sidewalk, then the street. My mother is upstairs because last night she did not sleep; she has been having trouble sleeping. My father is away as he often is away: business. My brother is on the other side of the neighborhood creek with friends who are not me. My sister is playing in the room we share, and so, for now, it is quiet.

This leaves us to us, my uncle and me.

Catching the light.

Replicating beauty.

At Bonwit's, they will sell what we have made. At Barney's. At Neiman's. At the fancy places my uncle goes in his quiet shoes and soft-checkered suits—tall suits because he is so tall, bright ties because he is not like other men; no other men are so fancy. He covers his smile with his Elmer's hand when he laughs. He writes to movie stars. He shops flea markets for the gifts he chooses just for me, using newsprint to wrap them with, leftover velveteen ribbon. Sometimes, he forgets to give me the gift that he found and wrapped and drove all that way, two hours. And then his hand scrapes the bottom of a busted paper bag, and he looks up and he smiles. Remembers.

Upstairs, outside, elsewhere: others. No one but us at the table that creaks, paper bags at our feet, the crumpled wells of our affection, the proof of what we made, and someday, someday, this will be it—his material as my memory, our history as my tone.

Groceries, sure. New clothes, Goodwill clothes. Books borrowed from the library, books donated to book sales. Wine bottles. Gifts. Walking shoes, a toothbrush and a change of clothes, the rolls of coins you are taking to the teller. Anything that is too much for two hands, too informal for a suitcase, too spur of the moment, just routine. Also: flat, snapped open, free as a kite in the breeze, or puffed up and out for homemade puppetry, or laid down in defense of your third-grade science book, which you will have to return at the end of the school year, without a scratch or scrape. Or your brother's mask: two holes for eyes, one giant oval for the mouth, cotton-ball ears. Or where next spring's bulbs are kept.

It all started with Francis Wolle and his 1852 design of the first machine that could mass-produce a rather slender paper bag. Not much to it. You could fit some air in there. Some letters. Maybe some banana leaves.

But it was Margaret E. Knight, who, after leaving school at the age of twelve to take a job at a New Hampshire textile mill and receiving no further education, would grow up to design the paper bag machine for the flat-bottomed bag—the frame, the gears, the cranks of the thing.

Knight was a born inventor. Better wooden toys for her brothers, faster sleds for the snow, a safety device for the looms in the mill where she'd gone to work to help her newly widowed mother pay the bills. It was while working on the assembly line at the Columbia Paper Bag company that she began to sketch, and then refine, a prototype for a paper bag machine.

When a con man stole and replicated her sketches, when he claimed that no woman could have invented such a thing, Knight took him to court and won—spending more money than an assembly-line worker is supposed to have on the legal team who would defend her. After that, she patented her paper bag machine—July 11, 1871, #116,842—and after that, she sought and received paper bag machine licensing fees and royalties, opened her own paper bag factory, and received from the queen of England the decoration of the Royal Legion of Honor. When she died at age seventy, she was still at work, conjuring new things the world might need. Twenty hours a day, says her *New York Times* obituary. Her eighty-ninth invention.

The paper bag is unassuming, it's self-effacing, it is anything we want it to be, most anything we need, and we can thank a woman for the ease of its assembly, its mass-making, its cheapness. Our histories deep in the well of it. Our varnished intimacies.

Amateur Art

February is white as a sanatorium, and only the violas bloom from their paper bag on the sill, knocking each other out in a patch of tenderized sunlight.

I settle the pain in my head by remembering the butterfly I once drew all the one day and then the next, until its wings were a stained-glass firmament and its antennae fuzzed the way real antennae do. Not being in any way blessed, the butterfly rose, in my estimation, to art, to my first best exercise in conceit and self-promotion, so much so that wherever I went for a week, two weeks, I carted the winged creature and explained myself through it.

Funny how the barest trace of it remains these fifty-odd years on, the chiaroscuro of those wings, launched even now into the still white hull of winter.

It was our proper fresh start, our next best. No scraps, yet, on the floor. No missing colors. Anything imaginable infinitely possible with the aid of blunt-force scissors, wells of watercolor, glue slime, Magic Markers, crayons, tape. Our uncles bought it at the drugstore. Our neighbors had an extra stash. Our teachers in their low, comfortable heels or slightly stained neckties disappeared into the supply closet and then came back. Voilà:

A virgin pad of construction paper.

Do with it what we may. Hatch the paper chains, the butterfly, the partner history project, the cone we pressed to our lips like a bullhorn to win the argument with our sister. Construction paper was the moment of our moments, destined to fade, tear, buckle, to become, in the words of art conservator Joan Irving, its own "history of impermanence."

And yet, the nineteenth-century factories and educators that introduced this wood chip–pulp product into kindergarten classrooms had something more permanent in mind—the teaching of color theory, for example, and the happy instructions of "gifts," a concept that had been put forth by the German Friedrich Froebel (1782–1852), a nineteenth-century educational reformer who believed that play lies at the heart of learning, and what is play if not (at least in part) cutting, punching, folding, weaving, and stitching paper? By the late nineteenth century, paper manufacturers were adapting their machinery to meet the demand, and soon such artists as the Siberian-born, New York City transplant Abraham Walkowitz (1878–1965) were playing with the paper, too, not concerning themselves with the problems of impermanence that art conservators like Irving would one day face.

We have our own problems, of course, with impermanence. With the oceanic life poster that, all these years later, represents the deep of the sea as a sepia stain. With the cotton ball–accented cloudscapes that have faded to gray. With the cards we made for our mothers all those years ago, no longer exuberant in their soft and placid pinks, no longer winning her attention. We launch our paper wings in memory now. We steal our memory from the fade.

Saturation

Your love for color was like your love for words: You hardly understood such things, but you preferred them saturated. You were blithe around the margins of your wide-ruled filler paper. You obliterated the angles in your father's quarter-inch graph paper. You brought excessive force upon the thirty-pound newsprint that lay before you on the floor, your elbows carpet-burned and the stomach of your cotton T-shirt slicked with summer sweat. You wanted maximum chroma from your azure blue, carnation pink, and goldenrod. You wanted rhyme inside your sentences and the sweet, stuffed excess of too many syllables per word. Presupposing and exaggerating, watercoloring your paper before you burrowed poems within, you drew invisible half circles in the air with your naked toes as you worked and broke straight through the page.

Only the spirograph got you to behave, the plastic machinery of roulette curves. The spirograph was a game of gears. You pinned a toothy stator to your page, then chose a wheel that fit inside, then slipped the tip of a pen into a hole in the wheel, and then, with a steady and unrebellious hand, circled your wheel (the plastic teeth on its exterior rim biting the teeth of the stator) as a flower or a Milky Way star or some new-breed geometric shape bloomed on your page. It was a miracle every time, unless your wheel's teeth lost their alignment. Barely capable of repeating yourself, you hollered praise at your creations. Blue loops. Red oblongs. Hypotrochoids. Epitrochoids.

Years later, in the thick of the pandemic, you attended to your hurt with more blazing saturation. Cadmium Yellow. Terre Verte. Raw

Sienna. Teal. Titanium White. Effervesce of Copper. Your father had died, his feathers had flown, and despair had broken through, and that is why you ordered Golden Opens, which came in a box that bumped the front door when it landed. Cool, wide tubes. A little resistance in the caps, and then the colors, wet and thick, actual, uncompromised, defiant. You pressed color coins onto a Gelli plate. You smashed the coins with a brayer. You tore leaves off trees and pressed them into the effervescence, then rubbed the proof onto fifty-pound white sulphite. Then, you bound what you made into something you could hold. Awl pierce, needle scratch, wax thread, the beginning and the end of color.

You subsisted on acrylic possibilities while your grief raged on. You located your childhood in color. Teal was the community pool at the edge of the day where your chlorine-saturated father swam off the smells of the job at the refinery, while you sat, watching. Cadmium Yellow was the glaze of dawn on winter ice and the '67 Dodge Dart that your father drove, both of you silent and careful on the slick. Terre Verte was the frost that dimmed the path in the garden called Longwood, where you and your father walked toward the sound of a fountain overspilling. Gold was you by the sea beside your father, watching the sun do its casting.

White was the unmarked sheet of paper that your father lay before you. It was the precursor to your own saturation.

Is the making head or heart? Are the hands first speech?

Nicholas-Louis Robert (1761–1828), the French mechanical engineer who invented the world's first machine that could, to quote Jules Heller, "make paper in an endless web, as wide as the machine he devised," would find himself on the losing end of patent litigation and, following a late-stage career as a school teacher, die impoverished. Still, he'd set ubiquity in motion, making way for the massive fourdrinier machine that would one day inundate the world with easy paper.

The fourdrinier machine has four primary zones: the wet end (into which a slurry of bark-free pulp is fed and then refined with sizing and color, among other things); the press section (where water is squeezed from the pulp); the dryer (which, through heat, further dries and stretches the paper); and the calender (through which the paper is rolled and further pressed into its factory finish). The finished product sits coiled into its tambour—a giant roll—until it is sliced and wrapped and shipped.

Easy paper is tabula rosa paper—virginal and unaffected by the human touch. Every sheet in the ream is essentially the same. Every specification is repeatedly met. You will not find, as paper historian and maker Timothy Barrett speaks of finding in early-century paper, an errant, embedded thumbprint on your page. No spots of rust. No squiggle of lost hair. You won't find what Dard loved best—proof of a hand-held deckle and mold, a hardwired watermark.

I never gave it all a second thought—not when I was a child saturating, spirographing. Poeming. Paper came from the store, or I received it as a gift, and after that it belonged to me—my canvas, my white wall, my liberator, my talk.

Nothing could have been more simple.

Oatmeal Box

I was ready for my great experiment—the making of a pinhole camera. My accomplice was a teacher. According to my careful, cursive, fourth-grade report, topped by fluorescent, hand-lettered cover-page calligraphy and secured by curly-ribbon binding:

> Then Mrs. Champion drew me a diagram on a piece of paper on how you make a pinhole camera. These were the directions:
>
> 1. find an empty oatmeal box with the top
> 2. cut a hole about as big as a dough-nut center in the bottom
> 3. find a piece of foil about 2 square inches long and tape the foil over the hole
> 4. now stick a pin through the middle of the foil
> 5. now find a piece of cardboard about 2 × 3 inches long and put tape at the ends.
> 6. make sure everything is concealed because if it isn't light-tight your pictures won't turn out
>
> After I had done all this, I took my camera to Mrs. Champion, and she proof-checked. Mrs. Champion said that my camera was good but that I should line the inside for a better picture. I lined my pinhole camera with black construction paper, and then my camera was good for taking pictures.
>
> On Thursday afternoon, I went over to Mrs. Champion's house. In her darkroom, we taped photographic paper on my pinhole lid, and I was ready to start.

> Now came the hard part—to pick my scene. We had to find a place with enough sunlight, and finally we did. The place I picked was a place with a pot of flowers. This pot of flowers was going to be my first pinhole picture. . . .
>
> My first picture did not turn out too good because there was not enough light. In my second picture, I overexposed it, and my negative didn't turn out too well. In my third picture, I put the photographic paper on the wrong side, and nothing turned out. But finally I took a perfect picture, and it turned out very good.

I wonder whether I waited until the Quaker Oatmeal box was empty or whether I—dramatic with impatience—poured the extra dusty flakes into the trash and hid the evidence. I don't wonder whether I traveled to Mrs. Champion's house with haste, for I see myself now riding the great speed of my Schwinn, throwing bike tricks on the downhill slopes, and leaving my hair in tangles.

Mrs. Champion was getting her master's degree in photography, and I was eager for her teaching. At her command, I filled my project book with the history of the camera, the chemistries of the processing baths, and the precise number of seconds that ticked as I (a frisson of hope passing, a heartbeat of worry) exposed the photographic paper to the light. I learned a new definition for *metamorphosis*, which is to say the conversion of a Quaker cardboard cylinder into a tool for art. I learned what power might be mine if I could pay attention, be a student, convert an empty nothing into something.

You finish with a box, and what you have is a box: new, capable, and multivalent. A second chance. A perfect picture. Trash as paradox.

Cheerios. Saltines. Barilla. Uncle Ben's. Rigatoni. Cracker Jacks. Wheaties. Honey Bunches of Oats. Those Quakers.

The boxes and cartons that fed us also taught us to read, to ask questions, to root for champions, to worry over missing children, or to search for hidden charms. They were to be emptied, and when they were, we had a choice: to toss them cavalierly or to make them new again.

It is necessary to stop, to say it: All that paper is (when not cotton, linen, plant-based) all those trees, is all that water in and out, that energy and smoke rise, the sickening smell of sulfur that filled the car as your father drove beneath the Spanish moss of South Carolina and through invisible fumes.

Dad, what is *that?*

Just hold your breath.

But what is it?

That's paper.

You could say that recycling lies at the historic heart of papermaking—tear those old sheets, mash those old linens, pulp the trash, add water, squeeze, lift, dry. But every process has its evolved chemistries, machines, and greed; every process wreaks its havoc; and the truth is that for far too many years, industrial paper manufacturers made their paper without regard for the landscapes that they sullied. They knocked the forests down, stripped the trees, ground the wood chips, and added heat and chemicals until the pulp was ready for the papermaking machines, which required more energy, more water, more chemicals to get the job down. Paper recycling—while far kinder to the environment—is not impact-free. You can't release the fibers of the recycled paper or the residual adhesives and ink without industrial quantities of water, heat, and chemicals. Nor can paper be perpetually recycled; at one point, the released fibers have no more binding strength.

According to the World Wildlife Fund, the pulp and paper industry represents 13% to 15% of global wood consumption. According to *The World Counts* website, ten liters of water are required to produce just one sheet of A4 paper, while "each tonne of recycled paper can avoid the use of 17 trees; 1,440 liters of oil; 2.3 cubic meters of landfill space; 4,000 kilowatts of energy and 26,500 liters of water." Managing our resources—replanting forests, using more of the whole tree in the process, reusing water supplies, diminishing the toxicities of chemicals, recycling more aggressively, among other things—has become a top priority for leading paper manufacturers, engineers, and such organizations as the Forest Stewardship Council and the Union of Concerned Scientists. And the impact of paper manufacturing and disposal is, of course, different and in some ways kinder than the environmental impacts of machines and plastics and batteries and the special metals that power our phones, our innovations, our artificial remembering.

Still, denuded forests feed our toilet-paper habit, paper arrives by the ton to our landfills, water runs scarce, and time is not on our side.

According to Sue Gosin, who grew up among a commercial papermaking family and cofounded the nonprofit collaborative hand-papermaking institution Dieu Donné, a forest tree doesn't want to be paper. A forest tree wants to stand straight, reach for the sky. Perhaps someday, she says, the commercial paper manufacturers will turn their sights on corn husks, blackberry vines, cattails, raffia, yucca, mugwort, wheat straw—on all the fibrous harvests, in other words, that would be kinder to our planet. More alkaline. Less acid. More shade.

In the meantime, a friend collects the trash of New York City and churns it into paper. The artist Samuelle Green fashions cones from paper that has been tossed aside and, securing one cone beside another, builds deeply dimensional installations, so that those who wander in and through might imagine themselves inside a stalactite cave or a honeycomb. In our households, in our businesses, we increasingly swap our thinking for bits and bytes, and share our truths in thumb drives, and trash our letters and our evidence in virtual cans. Even so, paper remains. Each sheet, each ream, each box—ubiquitous and precious.

Home

Dear Dard:

Once, for an entire semester at Penn, I taught home. I wanted to know what home is. Was? I asked the students to tell me. Reading George Hodgman's *Bettyville*, Michael Ondaatje's *Running in the Family*, Helen Macdonald's *H Is for Hawk*, reading their own photographs, reading what they could remember, they began to tell me. Home was a white Volkswagen Jetta. Home was a vessel of *prang*. Home was where boredom was tolerated. Home was anything but a noun. Home was a question. Home was the kitchen, but also the shower. Home was an ideal that had to be left before it could be idealized.

Their words, Dard. Their genius.

You? Home was a house near a river, your father's *News-Advertiser*, the Buckeye Wizard's traveling stage, the New Glenwood Hotel, the rail line to Buffalo, the roil of Roycroft, the dry weather of Cuernavaca, the two rooms in Vienna infused with the perfume of bakery bread, the view in London, the old Marlborough house "located in a hollow almost surrounded by heavily wooded hills," the antique foundry in Lime Rock, the museum in Cambridge, a friend's place in San Juan, mostly all those million miles you traveled, and mostly (mostly) Mountain House, the oddity of the place built high on a Chillicothe hill by a German immigrant who wished to honor wine. Wine-bottle windows. Grape-growing terraces. A vault for all the good stuff.

When you bought the place in 1919, you had work to do. The floors were rotting. The walls were wavering. The natural light required amplification, and so you sliced off a quadrant of the second floor and cut a hole into the roof and filled that space with your ambition. It was there, Dard, that you made the books that helped make you, beginning with *Old Papermaking*, in 1923. Crank, page, crank, until that book was done and you began again, each book a complication and a dream, each one yours, and rare, and housed in museums now, or sold for thousands of dollars.

(Like Van Gogh, Dard. Your worth multiplying upon your passing.)

You raised your two sons at Mountain House (when you were home). You listened to Edith at her ivories in the square front room (when she wasn't off traveling herself). You stored your treasures and your letters and your ideas in nooks, built what you needed, and the thing is: You don't need me as your memory's echo chamber. You were there. You sat in the fatigue of those chairs. You stood in the silo of light that came in from above, you poured your cereal into a bowl you pulled from a wooden shelf, you fought your asthma in the humid air that stole in through the cracks in the windows. You protected your private life with humor.

But now, Dard. Now?

Mountain House is the home of the son of your son, Dard III, the legacy you did not live long enough to meet. He has been living in your world since he was two days old—occupying the spaces you left with his head, his hands, his heart. He sweeps the brick walk beneath the towering gingko. He locks your books and your letters inside the vault. He hangs your pith helmet (a gift from Gandhi) and faded lei (it is not purple) from the press you used, sets the type you forged, opens the house to those who ask, and I asked him, Dard. I was audacious. Just one more pilgrim in the pilgrimage to Dard. Just one more ordinary quester.

Curiosity as invasion.

But you belong not just to history but to family. But your house, now in your grandson's hands, is growing. It has more air; it breathes. He was a kid, Dard, when he crawled into the earth and dug a basement out with his own hands, dumping the dirt over the side of the hill and stacking concrete block to prevent a catastrophic structural topple. (*You have carte blanche*, your son told his son, and so he took it.) He was nineteen, his father newly and so terribly dead, when he exerted his grief against the floors, the rooms, the so many things. He learned to seam a roof from a magazine, reglazed the drafty windows, rearranged the furniture (but not your books), is fashioning a kitchen off the back brick wall—those are the cabinets he made, that is the floor he planed and laid, that will be the table he joins and sands from the pecan tree that once grew in your yard, and here he will soon be, digging with his own hands, among the roots of that most magnificent gingko, so that he might build a new front room where his wife and his cat and his dogs will sit in the light that filters in between the leaves.

Your grandson learned to cook in your old kitchen: Soufflé, he claims, is the kind of dish you think on, until its method finally occurs. He organized the letters you typed on your portable typewriter, you addressing your sons and your wife and your friends with their proper nicknames. Still young, he hosted, for three continuous years, your biographer, while she sorted your life in your bedroom, at your desk. He said yes to the inquiring, sought out the people of your past, secured your missing artifacts, which is to say that first Marlborough press and the other halves of your correspondence. He made your Art Deco new again—calling on artisans to translate your signature shapes and colors into teacups, pendants, welcome mats, tiles, cards, tissue paper. On a pair of polished shuffleboard tables in a ten-thousand-square-foot workshop in downtown Chillicothe, he oversees the fulfillment of orders and then pushes through paint-chipped doors and takes the irregular concrete stairs into the vast spaces where his frame-and-molding business is underway.

It is here, among big machines and sawn timbers, pots of stain and sheets of sandpaper, bags of sawdust and a crew of carpenters, where, I think, he is most at peace. It is here where he, rising for work at 3:30 A.M. each day, checks the hand-waxed patina on his quartersawn white oak, the joinery in his mortise and tenon frames, the problems that he converts into puzzles and, with your brand of ingenuity, solves. It is here where he remembers his father and, in remembering his father, remembers how his father remembered you.

The reverb of love, in your grandson.

And sometimes, when his rescue dog Homer seeks a reprieve from a sky full of Independence Day crackle, when the noise of the world crashes down upon them both, when he wants to be in touch with you, he retreats into the vault where your books still live and sits—Homer "beneath the safety of a flat file"—while he reads your diaries. You remain mysterious to him, Dard. His name is a repeat, and a question.

I have slipped inside the room where you died, in Mountain House. I have looked out beneath the stained-glass panes and through, to your final view of Chillicothe. I have watched your grandson pull a small, eggshell-colored, dark-tipped wand from a fireplace mantel and say, constructing each sentence before he speaks: *This will interest you: Phil's magic wand.* I have stood beneath the pale sun in your workroom while your grandson explained your way of making type, your way of composing, your way of pressing pages, one color at a time, the wet sheets clipped to a thin string with wooden clothespins. I have entered that vault where he keeps your books safe, your letters, the possibility of your secrets. I did not touch the crust of your lei or the rim of your pith helmet, and I saved your grandson no time at all, which is the only thing he will confess to wanting. Everything else, one might teach one's self. Everything else might be remembered.

Your Mountain House is your home, still, Dard. I can walk its halls. I cannot steal its secrets. I can only know home as the places where I lived, and even then, the mysteries are manifold.

Recipe

Food, yes—I'll use the clumsy word, forget the thesaurus substitutes. That wouldn't be me, to dress up her delicious with dictionary equivalents. It was just tender meat. It was just moist brownies. It was just fried smelts on Christmas Eve and triple birthday cakes on birthdays and sweet potatoes the color of glazed carrots on Thanksgiving. Her applesauce. Her strawberry preserves. Her peas in the stew, her cheese for the fondue, her checkerboard cookies, her sandwich cookies, her shortbread, her chocolate frosting.

If you were to be good at something, wouldn't you want to be good at this? She made the meals. She fed us. She checklisted our senses. The room where she cooked was the room where we thrived, and often I would watch her—skimming the magazines for something new, clipping the recipes, and stuffing them, loose, into her notebook. On the lined sheets of paper in that three-ring binder, she would write of her experiments with her looping left hand, neglecting to account for the temperature or the cook time, confusing tablespoons and teaspoons, pressing the back of her damp fist upon the page so that half of her blue letters receded—tidal and blurry.

This is no critique. She knew what she meant, intuited the proper, was not recipe-booking for history's sake, would not have imagined her oldest daughter coveting that notebook after she was gone, taking it, setting out the sifter and spoons, the cups and bowls, the chocolate and butter, the flour and sugar and walnuts and eggs and salt and extra double doses of vanilla, like an amateur hologrammer.

I miss the sticky wooden batter spoon that she made mine for the licking. I miss the frosting bowl that I wiped clean with my forefinger. I miss the pink in her roast beef and the red in her sauce and the yellow in her omelet. I miss the person I was before I stomped off into battle with my own attrition—repudiating her deliciousness for five long years so that I might stand among the armored anorectics.

Against her.

Against myself.

Now, in my small house, in my modest kitchen, her recipes fall loose from the old binder. Her blue-blurred pages jump their silver rings. On the backs of some of her pages, I find my brother's primary school math and my handwriting practice and a scribble of her thinking, which maybe was her wishing that she were reading books instead of writing recipes, that she were writing books instead of cooking, that she were good at something beyond the thing she was so very, very good at.

In this present hour, I guess the cook time. I estimate the temperature. I go half tablespoon and half teaspoon, and someday, maybe, I will get it right. I will put my notes beside her notes, and we will stand aligned, in the house where I live, where I am the mother now.

"Do you ever watch Jacque Pepin on PBS?" Dard Hunter III writes. "He had an important segment on cooking with children. He made a soufflé with his granddaughter."

"She thrust her hands in and kneaded the flesh, careful not to dislodge the bones," Chang-Rae Lee writes in "Coming Home

Again," about his mother, who is now dying, and her *kalbi*, which he must learn to cook. "I asked her why it mattered that they remain connected. 'The meat needs the bone nearby,' she said, 'to borrow its richness.'"

"Her small hand curves like eggshell: satin skin, round fingers, dimples in place of knuckles," writes Diana Abu-Jaber of her young inquisitive daughter, in *Life without a Recipe*. "The brown egg echoes her holding hand. My breath is there too, inside the curve of her holding, waiting for the crack."

You could say that a recipe is quantities, qualities, ingredients, more math, notes on expectations, preemptions for frustrations, instructions on when and how to touch. If this, then that. Room-temperature the eggs. Zest until there's dust. Don't overcream. Don't undersalt. Replace the lime with the lemon. Sift, but only once. As many slivered almonds as you want.

You could say that, but you'd be neglecting the history that recipes contain, the intensity and ardor. All that we lose when we lose our cook, the sound of their knife through the skin of the onion, the smells of their sauce on the stove.

Wendy Wall, a professor of humanities at Northwestern University who decided to write of recipes and their makers in England between 1575 and 1650, was really asking questions: "How could a recipe function simultaneously as scientific experiment and poetic exercise of wit? . . . In what precise ways did housewives contemplate figuration, natural philosophy, memory, and matter itself, even as they seemingly conformed to traditional and presumptively passive norms of female behavior? What did recipes allow people to explore, think, do, consider, make, and taste in the early modern period?"

Before recipes were recipes, they were "receipts," Wall says. They were as likely to address the savory and the sweet as they were to provide instructions on the making of medicines or, say, ink. They were "transit points" and "displays of skills," instructions embedded with mysteries and secrets, small masteries of ideology and faith that "probed what it meant to be a maker, knower, creator, artist, artificer, worker, and preserver in early modern terms and within spaces that included the *domus*."

Recipe reconstruction is the stuff of empathy and science, some deep detective skills. It's work for the enthusiast and the skilled. When, for example, Marissa Nicosia decides to "make a leach of dates," she handles the pages of history before she touches a single ingredient—reading deep into rare book rooms so that she might emerge, as she writes on her blog, *Cooking in the Archives*, with a banquet: "Naturally sweet from dates, elevated with sugar, scented with rosewater, and spiced with cinnamon and ginger, a tiny bite of this confection is immensely flavorful." Nicosia decodes fading handwriting and stained pages. She yields the edible concoction.

Today, so many recipes are brand, pretension, style. They are a *New York Times* link posted on Facebook. They are proofed by iPhone pictures texted to a friend in the high heat of a blackened oven's steam, a Twitter surge, a TikTok. But they are also challenges, dares, portals to the past, *our* past, if we can just pay attention to their nuance: Don't overcream. Don't undersalt. Don't trust the lime. Don't lay a damp fist down on your mother's blue ink. Don't wash her out to sea.

Paper Games

The smudged-smooth surface of the blanched card table. Sometimes the linoleum polish or carpeted plush of the floor. Rarely (but as we got older, more so) the kitchen table. We counted our paper money, struck our thimble upon Park Place, ceded Marvin Gardens, passed the cardboard GO. Also: Go Fish. Crazy Eights. Guess Who? Clue. Who won was always a test, proof of place in the nearest hierarchy, a corroboration of the luck or intelligence we might carry forward, into the darkening hours of the afternoon.

Dilated.

Deflated.

Game determined.

So that the other day, assembling a puzzle with my husband and my son—my husband jabbering each piece into place, my son resourceful and stoic, my heart ticking the song of anxious inadequacy as I triumphed less, and *silently*, I thought of all those years ago and how, in the memory of the houses where I once lived, I lose, and lose again.

A pleasure, a pastime, a puzzle, a game. But think of what it stirs in us. How many hours we have spent Solitaire-ing, moguling Boardwalk, tallying our scores, trying to complete the picture.

Our gamesmanship is noted, our gloating and our pouting. We are stratified by our relative wins, made world-ready by our paper tactics.

John Spilsbury, the mid-eighteenth-century British engraver who profited from the rise of global curiosity by producing educational "dissected puzzles" (here was Europe in its interlocking pieces; here, Asia, broken, without its bordering seas; here, Africa in brilliant hooked and jiggered tiles), would be dead by the age of thirty.

And yet his thin mahogany puzzle pieces and sliding-lid boxes would lay the groundwork for the cardboard puzzles and paper-bound board games that would be invented and mass-produced by later-century Americans, such as Milton Bradley; George S. Parker (picture, in Parker's factory, circa 1909, each worker cutting some 1,400 puzzle pieces a day); Herman, Hillel, and Henry Hassenfeld. It's their games we've played. Their games we've let define us: Sore loser. Brilliant strategist. Just lucky. Team player. On the up-and-up. A cheat.

Think of the enterprising Spilsbury the next time you pull a puzzle from the shelf, tip its contents, and search for the first snap. Or think of Lord Spencer's four-year-old son in the 1760s, who, thanks to Spilsbury and his comely puzzles, already knew

> *the situation of every kingdom, country, city, river, and remarkable mountains, in the world. For this attainment . . . he was indebted to a plaything, having been accustomed to amuse himself with those maps which are cut into several compartments, so as to be thrown into a heap of*

> *confusion, that they may be put together again with an exact coincidence of all their angles and bearings, so as to form a perfect whole.*

Puzzling and playing, mostly the perfect whole eludes us. But sometimes, miraculously, we find that exact coincidence of angles. We emerge triumphant, a momentary victor over our common imperfections.

Sewing Pattern

She has to take the measure of her daughter. The first one. The one with the coarse dark hair and the face that comes directly from her husband (the girl's father), except for the nose; the daughter has been spared the hook in the beak of her husband's nose.

(A son might have carried that nose, but, please, not a daughter.)

Still, spared the nose, the daughter has her deficits. More than anything, her acrid awareness of her many deficits. This knowing curved into the slump of her shoulder blades and into the stiff-legged way that she walks right up to the edge of things, where she will stop, no faith at all in her own physicality or charm, in her ability to expand a room by others' happiness to see her, except for when she is on the ice, when she is ice-skating.

First, on a Boston pond, the daughter skated. Then, on a rink in Wilmington, Delaware. Now, at the Philadelphia Humane Society in Ardmore, Pennsylvania, because the family has a new house now, a brand-new neighborhood. There, the daughter has acquired speed and a gritty, mystifying flair, a long leaping axle, double loops, double flips, and double lutzes (no double wallies, ever). She has the high-speed chase of the crossovers that accelerate toward the ecstatic flights across the ice, the dizzying spins (but never a successful layback), the crescendo diagonal slice of an Ina Bauer, the repertoire of footwork, which the daughter pretends to improvise, but it is always the same coalescence of mohawks, three-turns, brackets, arms up and hands graceful as a dainty woman dropping a dainty napkin.

(The daughter is never actually dainty. Only her hands are dainty, and only when she is on the ice, skating.)

All this the mother sees in the afternoons when she leaves the bright new home where she's been working and arrives to retrieve her daughter from the rink. Her daughter's program music playing over the rink's loudspeakers. Her daughter's archrival throwing her own double lutzes in her own chosen corners precisely when the daughter is toeing in and throwing hers. The mother stands in the numbing cold in her low-heeled shoes, her almost-opaque nylons, her plaid wool skirt, and her heavy coat. Stands there watching at the metal barrier—not as the fanciest of mothers but as the prettiest one: dark hair, big eyes, Pond's skin, fine nose. Stands there as a woman who left her business at home—a woman who sews, a woman perpetually taking the measure of her stubbornly self-crucifying daughter:

Back waist length

Bust line

Hip point

Inseam

Waistline

Mood

At home, in the alley of her sewing room—the Singer ensconced along the far short wall, pale yellow cabinets along the one long wall, a deep-silled window along the other long wall (plants in pots on the sill, the laundry line strung between tree and house just beyond)—the mother's latest pattern waits. A Butterick this time, the 5940 Young Junior/Teen Cheerleader, Majorette, and Skating Dress Costume, purchased after some deliberation for 85 cents at the local fabric and notions store. It's a "Fitted micro-mini dress with three collar variations and princess seaming, has flared skirt with or without contrast godets. Barrel cuffed full, full length sleeves or semi-fitted full length sleeves. With or without braid and button trim on shoulders, sleeves and dress front. Briefs, with back zipper closing, are elasticized at waistline and legs." According to the package.

The slightly beige tissue-paper pattern has fifteen pieces. It is a kind of map, a topography defined by fold lines and easing lines, darts and dots, squares and triangles, adjustment lines, seam allowances, notches. Days earlier, standing beneath the flicker-buzz of fluorescent lights, in the narrow aisles of the store, among bolts of color, yards of thread, temptations of trim, zippers and rickrack, Buttericks, Simplicities, McCalls, the mother had made her choices and then brought her purchases home, imagining the daughter out on the ice, wearing the costume she will make. With her own time. With her own surrender to a certain kind of love.

She is a good seamstress, this mother—boastlessly artful with skilled hands that slip the pattern from its package and lay it flat and, with silver scissors, snip. There will be globe-tipped pins in her teeth when she secures the fabric to the pattern. An iron hissing steam. The acid-free crinkle of that 85-cent pattern. There will be her history as a mother who has dressed both her daughters in clothes of her own making for almost as long as she has been a mother. Her room of her own is a room for their own:

Butterick 5041 Girls' One-Piece Dress of Jumper

Simplicity 7785 Girls Jumper Dress

Simplicity 7921 Drop Waist with Ribbon Belt

McCalls 9384 Child High Waist Flower Girl Dress

And, soon, the Butterick 5940 Young Junior/Teen Cheerleader, Majorette, and Skating Dress Costume

If only there were a different first daughter. One who did not shrink from life and what life might be but for there, at the rink, on the ice, where she (so much hubris) imagines herself as a someday champion, transformed into the likes of Janet Lynn, who should (the daughter thinks) have won every single medal in every single competition that she entered. Janet Lynn, who was once seen skating to Beethoven's Leonore Overture No. 3 while wearing a sleek pink costume, made by a professional tailor.

That is what the daughter wants, what the daughter believes will finally transform her—a skating costume made not by a mother and a Butterick, but by a *professional* tailor, by other hands and other eyes that take her measure. The daughter will not say the words out loud. Instead, she'll sulk in silence. But the mother knows, and her own mood and measure will darken, as, in days to come, she will smooth and cut that the pattern, pins between her teeth, the iron hissing.

Some called them gods, those paper sewing patterns. Hundreds of years ago, they were a worthy inheritance slipped from tailor father to tailor son. *Don't show anyone else. This is our secret.*

But it was a woman who, with the enterprising support of her progressive husband, engineered the first mass production and wily distribution of sewing patterns, both in the United States and abroad. She'd made herself sound French—Madame Demorest—but Ellen Louise Curtis (1824–1898) was, in fact, a native New Yorker, the daughter of a hatmaker, a once-flourishing milliner operating her own high-fashion establishment, and the second wife of a progressive widower, William Jennings Demorest.

It was as a newly married woman taking a slight sabbatical from work that Ellen had a thought while watching her maid cut out a dress from a brown-wrapping paper pattern. I like the way Ishbel Ross tells the tale in *Crusades and Crinolines: The Life and Times of Ellen Curtis Demorest and William Jennings Demorest*: "Why not patterns in thin paper that could be duplicated endlessly and distributed at small cost? Why not assemble the asserted segments for demonstration purposes? Mr. Demorest hastened the development of this idea. To him it was largely a problem in mathematics."

Why not, indeed? So that, soon enough, a small crowd had gathered outside the Demorests' Philadelphia home on Franklin Square, to bear witness to two dozen paper patterns on display in the couple's front parlor. Again, Ross is our guide:

> *Women in tartans, with wasp waists, wide sleeves and flying bowknots clustered around the narrow house and blocked the stairs and sidewalk. They were face to face with a provocative innovation at a time when the sewing machine was whirring its way to mass popularity.*

Soon, the Demorests were in Manhattan, operating an emporium that retailed the patterns alongside additional Demorest-curated must-haves. By 1860, Mr. Demorest was launching *Mme. Demorest's Mirror of Fashions*, a quarterly publication with a blue and gold cover that both advertised the patterns—retailing for 25 cents, 50 cents, or even $1, depending on the type of garment and the relative complexity of the trim—and included a "free" sample pattern in every issue. In short order, the Demorests were hiring designers, further adapting French fashions to American tastes, catering to women of more or less means, and placing additional advertisements in such publications as *Frank Leslie's Ladies Gazette of Fashions* and *Godey's Lady's Book*. They sold the patterns not just in their own emporium but through "clubs" established across the United States, where African American sales agents worked side by side with white agents, received the same wages, and went to the same parties.

(The Demorests would prove to be exceedingly important abolitionists, following the decline of their pattern business.)

The Demorests didn't patent their patterns, but Ebenezer Butterick patented his—which gave him a distinct commercial advantage. Still, by 1876, the Demorests had sold more than three million paper patterns, had overseen an expansion to some 1,500 distribution shops, and were exhibiting in the Main Hall of the 1876 Philadelphia Centennial Exposition. You can see the madame's expert touch in the silver alum Centennial print that persists today—the mannequins adorned in Demorest fashions, the wooden showcases abundant with Demorest shirts and skirts, the drawers stuffed with the plenty of Demorest patterns.

Madame Demorest was an outspoken feminist—her paper patterns were designed to liberate the woman by placing coveted trendy fashions within economical reach. But by the time my mother was standing in a fabric and notions store, thumbing through the available patterns and choosing the accompanying fabrics, home-sewn clothes were simply not as commanding, in the eyes of at least one sullen American daughter, as the stuff that could be bought off the racks or fabricated by *professional* tailors.

Map

We left home by way of the Sunoco Gas roadmaps, which lost their crisp folding lines the moment they were unfolded. They made such pretty pictures, flipped to the traveling side—the primary fields of color, the decorative compass, the dashed lines for the scenic routes, the heavy continuum of highways.

The names of the places we were bound for.

In the back of the car, there were three of us, and, if we were all getting along, if our father had already studied the thing, if our mother said *yes*, the map was our thin blanket. Over our knees. Fingers as pointers. We could follow along, or we could detour our imaginations with the inset promises of state parks and local features.

Where would we have gone, without our maps? How would we have ever arrived? How do we each remember the backs of our legs sticky in the brand-new Dodge Dart and the perfumery of gasoline wafting up from the map that wouldn't snap back into its crisp folds? How do we imagine that we would have ever returned, found our way back home, and into the house, where a calico cat was waiting for us, the rooms we knew best, our Monopoly board, our games of hearts, our mother's cooking?

"Isn't writing, like remembering, a wayfaring? Aren't maps our way back, and our way forward?" writes Peter Turchi in *Maps of the Imagination: The Writer as Cartographer*:

The earliest maps are thought to have been created to help people find their way and to reduce their fear of the unknown. We want to know the location of what we deem life-sustaining (hunting grounds and sources of fresh water, then; now utility lines and grocery stores) and life-threatening (another people's lands; the toxic runoff from a landfill). Now, as then, we record great conflicts and meaningful discoveries. We organize information on maps in order to see our knowledge in a new way. As a result, maps suggest explanations; and while explanations reassure us, they also inspire us to ask more questions, consider other possibilities.

To ask for a map is to say, "Tell me a story."

Sheet Music

Take the sacred as Christmas Eve. My brother, standing tall and dirty blonde and thin behind my seated, auburn father. My brother playing his oboe, my father his piano.

Good King Wenceslas and the snow lay round.

Certain poor shepherds in the deep.

A little town where dark streets shineth.

The divine high C-sharp.

Lower the lights to a dim. Let my brother nod, and let him breathe; his oboe reed will sweeten. Let my father run his fingers up and down the Steinway keys, his right hand rising, quick, to flick the music forward; his left hand, with his gold wedding band, kept faithful to its octave.

Nothing lost. Holy gained. My father and my brother. They play: staff and clefs. Treble and bass. Notes stemmed and flagged, whole and halved and quartered, dotted, tied. My brother growing thinner. My father's foot working the softening, sustaining pedals, and, again, my brother breathes, and my father lifts his hand.

Flick.

The air is salty with the after-fry of smelts. The tree is heavy with adornment. The stockings are hung by the chimney with care.

There is a father and a son and their sheet music. There are two sisters and a mother.

Keep the memory whole. Uncomplicated. Don't leave this home for any other.

Sometimes a song just is—in the breast of a bird, in the drift of a whale, in the flap of wet sheets on a line, in a garage band's riff.

Alternatively: sheet music.

In 1853, John Mason Neale and Thomas Helmore penned their lyrics to a thirteenth-century tune and "Good King Wenceslas"—permanently scored—slipped among us and stayed. A few years later, Phillips Brooks, newly returned from the holy land, wrote "O Little Town of Bethlehem" for the children of Holy Trinity Church, in Philadelphia. Once theirs, it is now ours—not to keep but to render.

The first musical arrangement scored expressly for the United States emerged from the imagination of Alexander Reinagle, a British transplant, one-time friend of Bach, Mozart aficionado, sonata crafter, and tutor of George Washington's step-granddaughter. Reinagle, according to music historian John Bewley, became "perhaps the musician who most influenced musical taste and development in Philadelphia in the late 18th century." Commissioned to commemorate the ratification of the U.S. Constitution, Reinagle delivered a tune fit for fifes, horns, drums, quick fingers, and well-soled feet. A tune that could rise on a flag-whipping day and be carried on the back of a parade.

And it was.

At 8:00 A.M., on the morning of July 4, 1788, the grand affair began to take its one-and-a-half-mile-long shape at the intersection of Philadelphia's South and Third Streets. There, in predetermined stratifications, all varieties of spectaculars assembled—merchants and traders, farmers and makers, sign painters, brick layers, coach painters, spinning wheel makers, blacksmiths and whitesmiths, skinners and glovers, printers, bookbinders, stationers, whip and cane makers, tailors, instrument makers, brewers, barber-surgeons, sugar refiners, judges, politicians, horses of noble colors and fine grooming. Bearing feathery plumes and the artifacts of their manifold crafts (along with the weight of some truly epic constructions), the assembled citizens of the brand-new country lifted their knees and processed, taking their north–souths and east–wests within the orchestral hold of Reinagle's "Federal March."

By the time the parade massed and dissolved on the green slopes of William Hamilton's Bush Hill, copies of Reinagle's "Federal March" were being sold in the shops of Philadelphia merchants—scores of scores to be passed down among American generations, so that it might still be played today, and sometimes is.

Deed

It sat on the hill on the curve of the road. It had taken the shape of my father's graph-paper sketches and my mother's suggestions (a laundry chute through which to toss our Carter underwear; a sewing room; a fireplace in the family room; a downstairs master-bedroom suite, which would prove to be her best invention). It was a dusky sage color in the early years, and the front door was double-wide, with stained-glass insets. Inside, a chandelier hung. There were deep sills in the bow windows, flocked wallpapers, proper curtains, as much color as my mother wanted, an island in the kitchen with a collapsible counter that stood on two wobbly legs. Enough cabinetry for the recipes she stowed in three-ring binders.

Then, all the years went by. Then, she was dying in the glass box that had been built just past the mauve dining room. Like a greenhouse, that room was, with a view of the thicket of trees beyond and, late at night when the skies were clear, the moon. She never opened her eyes in her final days. I sang to her. My brother played her hymns on his recorder.

After she was gone, the house was many times too big. My father kept her orchids growing, went out for dinner, mostly let me clean. But all around him, my mother's things kept growing—the newspaper news that she'd collected, the Christmas cards she had received, the sewing patterns she had kept, despite their history. There were the books she'd bought in all their vaunted first editions: Maxfield Parrish. F. Scott Fitzgerald. Jack London. Ulysses S. Grant. Sinclair Lewis. The undisclosed Dard Hunter. There were the pages of something she had been writing, a project she had kept hidden.

It took ten months for us to dislodge, displace, undo her things when, nine years on, it came time for my father to leave. It was day upon day, until there was less of her in the house where she'd lived and more of her in memory. Finally, the house a hollow, my father and I stood side by side, surprised and saddened by what we'd achieved.

Not long afterward, in a shiver of a room on a sluice of a day, my father and I sat with the brand-new family and released the deed.

But does it ever really belong to us? That scratch of earth beneath the office window where we plant the elephant-ear bulb, pull the creep of weeds? That house with the chair by the window with the view? We fence it, lock it, secure it, sweep and rearrange it, color it ours, but someday, we will have no claim at all.

It's the deed that lives on, a convention traced to thirteenth-century Scotland, where the transfer of land from one to another was marked by a gift, an earthen token. The custom evolved. In England, there emerged the "Rituals of Turf and Twig." In Colonial America, there were bewildering "negotiations" with Native Americans. By 1795, the U.S. Congress had passed a law that required counties throughout the land to establish offices in which property deeds might be recorded.

The story of a deed will always be bigger than the story of a person. A deed is a pair of parentheses. But it is never the end of the sentence.

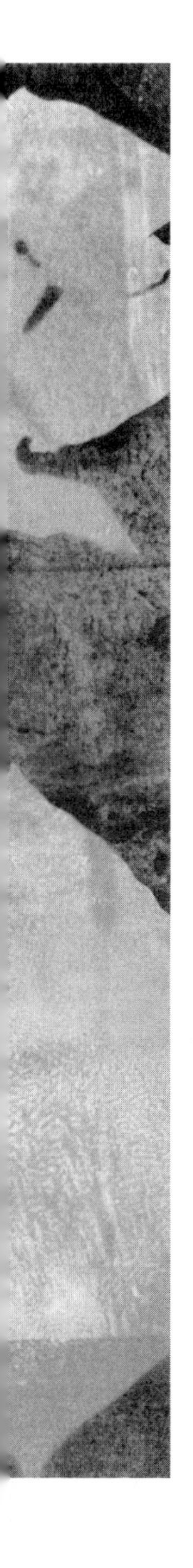

Obsession

Dear Dard:

Memoir is the original obsession vessel. That's what I say when I teach. It's that "kind of true story that operates as a container for the writer's preoccupation or crush, fascination or infatuation. That narrative arising from an *idée fixe* that claws itself into the writer's brain and stays, that scratches itself into sentences and metaphors, that maintains its grip on the frame."

I grow obsessed with your obsession, Dard. You, and your obsession, are emerging as my frame.

Sometimes, an obsession is a wind-whipped storm; at the center of the frenzy is a hush. Sometimes, it branches, dendritical, furcating into tangents without losing its momentum. Sometimes, it goes along and goes along, rounding its own corners, sneaking past snags, like a river not quite banking during a saturated spring. An obsession has roots, or an obsession has leaves.

Your obsession, Dard, was chemical, an alloy, a compositing of elements, each one a bit like fate. You were ushered into the life you built; I want to say that you were made for it. Hands and heart, body and feet, parental proclivities and ancestral genetics. You were the boy born into a newspaper family, your fingers stained early with ink. Your first talents were cartoons, chalk plates, illustrations, wood carving, long travels, horse taming, seed planting, best-brotherhood. Your father's library featured the work of the arts and crafts polymath artist William Morris, as well as a butcher paper–wrapped magazine produced by the philosopher-pastor Elbert Hubbard. Oddly coifed and remarkably strange, wearing the flop of a long tie at his neck and delighting in a company of idiosyncratic "cranks," Hubbard had built an artisan community in East Aurora, New York, called Roycroft, modeling the whole thing after a Morris workshop, although Roycroft was, according to Morris's own daughter, May, a dreadfully poor imitation.

(She would someday tell *you* that; you would someday meet her.)

Nevertheless:

You wanted to *see*. You ached to *do*. You had those hands, those feet.

By the age of nineteen, you were an unhappy special student at Ohio State. You would have gone off to London but couldn't afford the fare, so you boarded a train for Buffalo, New York, instead, setting your sights on those Roycrofters. They had no need for the help you offered, but you persisted, you charmed, you demonstrated your manual ingenuity. Soon, you were dropping out of Ohio State to become a Roycrofter through and through. Converted an old East Aurora cottage into your workshop. Learned the craft trades. You installed one of your own stained-glass patterns into the hotel windows and then, dissatisfied, smashed those windows with a hammer (it was winter; it was cold) and started all over again. You bound a widow's book in the tanned skin of her dead husband's back (it was her idea; you acquiesced). You sat with Eugene Debs, Clarence Darrow, William Wallace Denslow, and Margaret Sanger, pondering the country's fate. You met the woman you would marry, somehow seduced her (*How* did you seduce her? Why can't you say?). East Aurora was your proving ground. You left. You returned. You left. You returned. You one day brought your sons to visit. And then you did not return again.

By 1911, you were, for the second time, in Vienna, a center of graphic superiority. While your wife took piano lessons (she was a true talent, Dard, music being *her* obsession) and read novels and made the most of your clutch of borrowed rooms (Edith was the one making the most of things), you attended courses at the K. K. Graphische Lehr- und Versuchsanstalt. Getting into the school had required a fabricated diploma. Leaving, you had a real diploma in hand, but not one you believed that you deserved. You moved to London to gain work and respectability as a designer for the Norfolk Studios, but working for another was never quite your thing. You preferred to walk the streets, to sit in the bowels of the Victoria and Albert Museum and the old Science Museum, to listen to book people talk, to watch them work, to stalk the ghost of William Morris. Your London was innocent of war. Your London opened its doors to you, until you found yourself in a papermaker's basement, molding and couching for the first time. Everything that had been building in you had been building *this* you, until, upon the passing of more years, more travels and adventures, your ambition had been discharged into a vision:

> The work of the English private presses was of keen interest to me, and I felt I should like to attempt something of the kind myself. I was convinced, however, that simply purchasing type from a commercial foundry and buying paper from a paper mill left too many of the vital steps of making books in the hands of disinterested workmen. It was my desire to have my own private press, but I wanted my work to be individual and personal, without reliance upon outside help from the type founder or papermaker. I would return to America and attempt to make books by hand completely by my own labor—paper, type, printing.

Your obsession, Dard, was not a storm, it was not dendritical, it was not gently flowing, curving. It was, it seems to me, preordained and perpetually irresistible, a periodic table, a tabular arrangement, and if I choose to explain you like that, to shape your obsession vessel with the arrogance of my inquiry, how do I explain myself to the lovely, former student (profound and witty and talented, Dard; I think you'd really like her) who just yesterday stood beside me in Kislak while I turned your pages for her? She had questions, Dard, about what makes paper obsession worthy. She read your grandson's words on the sly, while I was talking to another. She said, *Really?* when I mentioned the afternoon you spent in the company of Gandhi. She honored your photographs. She asked questions about my pursuit. About how it began and where it is going. About the shape and weight of my vessel. About whether I am becoming a storm or a river, a seed or a root, a tree in bloom or a tree in autumn, dropping my own leaves.

We are our idiosyncrasies, our obsessions.

We all need to be forgiven.

I am a woman born to a family of obsessives. I am an obsessive obsessed with obsessives.

Listen, Dard.

Blueprints

If I begin with purple cabbage as the *prima facie* evidence, I must also begin with midnight, with me, my brother, my sister, our parents stiffened by a long car ride. Also here at the beginning is a white yapper of a toy poodle named Candy, and a bright light, such a bright light, bulbed above a dining-room table in a horizontal home at the foot of a hill in Tarrytown, New York.

For hours now, this cabbage, this yapper, this light have been waiting. Our father got a late start, there was traffic, but our great-aunt Ann in her sensible shoes and business suit is impervious to the prospect that cabbage and ham and pepper hash lose their appeal (if ever they had appeal) after the 10:00 P.M. hour. We are seated. Candy nips. Aunt Ann (we call her that) serves.

I sit facing the china-cabinet wall and train my thoughts on the Boehm porcelain—the mountain lion with the red poppy, the bunny with the spots, the crispy-petaled rose. If I study these things, if I wonder about them deeply, I will not taste the midnight cabbage or the hash. I will get through this meal, to the room beyond, where Aunt Ann's husband (we call him Uncle Lloyd) has hung the famous painting of his famous work. Uncle Lloyd is a major architect. He is the engraver's son who slipped off to Paris and then brought his beaux arts vision home to the jazz-age firm of Schultze and Weaver, which is the on-record architect of the Hotel Pierre, the Sherry-Netherland, the Miami Biltmore, Montauk Manor, the Breakers, and, of course, the Waldorf-Astoria of Park and Lexington.

Uncle Lloyd's famous painting has a title—*Buildings Designed by Schultze and Weaver, Architects, from 1921 to 1936*—and it is as long and nearly as tall as the wall beyond this room. The painting gleams and just slightly cracks, and I worry, as I try not to gag on the cabbage, that some of its gleam will have fallen away since the last time our family made the three-hour drive.

We eat assisted by sterling silver and linen napkins. We eat pretending that Candy has not peed on the piles of paper news in the corner of the kitchen, that we do not smell the smell. Uncle Lloyd is not among us. He is elusive. That's what obsession does, concludes my teenage self—it takes you away from people, it puts family at a distance, it puts the want in future storytellers. My brother and I will have to sneak around early tomorrow morning if we want to see the basement where all the blueprints live, that yellow trace, those triangles and pencils. Maybe Uncle Lloyd will be there, in the basement, while our parents and our sister sleep. Maybe he'll tell us about paper, or about the things that keep him out of reach.

Buildings Designed by Schultze and Weaver, Architects, from 1921 to 1936 is a brave new world, with a dark mahogany sky, and a landscape of sandstone-colored buildings all set out in tiered rows, and a lake of some kind, or a reflecting pool, so that the buildings appear twice—once upright, with plenty of dark sky for their halos, once downright and interestingly truncated.

The Waldorf-Astoria takes center stage. Built on the site of a former power plant and YMCA, built above the railway tracks of New York Central, the hotel itself was, I will read later, in a story written by Andrew S. Dolkart and published by *The Journal of Decorative and Propaganda Arts*, "the world's largest and tallest hotel, a building with a massive footprint, complex structural requirements, vast service areas, transient and semi-transient rooms, apartment suites, facilities for the Junior League and Canadian clubs, restaurants, lounges, a multistory ballroom, and function rooms of various sizes." The Waldorf-Astoria was, I will later read, in a book by Ward Morehouse III, clad inside with 1,585 cubic feet of Belgian black marble, 600 cubic feet of Italian Brech Montalto, and 360 cubic feet of Italian Alps Green and three hundred antique mantles, while its forty-seven-story façade presented eight hundred thousand cubic feet of limestone, which equaled two hundred railroad carloads, and then there was the matter of the "2,595,000 square feet of terra cotta and gypsum block" and the fact that it was built at the height of the Depression.

The Waldorf-Astoria all began, I will later think, with paper. A floor-plan sketch, an elevation, a cartoon, a set of blueprints where the rules were made and rolled and then unrolled, flopped down, sweated through, smudged. A rock to keep the plans from blowing in the wind between the columns of steel between the highest unbuilt windows.

But when I am there in that house, it is the painting itself that seems unquantifiable. All those tiny brushstrokes across all those complex facades, all those windows, all those doors, all those tiers, all those reflections, all the sky-high stones and mansard roofs and pinnacles, ever ascending. I wish that Uncle Lloyd would come to us and save us with a story.

Once, in a bit of fiction I wrote after Uncle Lloyd had died, I reincarnated him as a ghostly vision—ivory feet, ivory ankles, ivory arms, a white shirt, white pants, white hair thick and rumpled, neck the color of bone. I turned him into a man who led my brother and me out onto a roof so that we might dangle our feet in the night air, a man who afterward vanished. The story was like a dream, and the dream was like a memory, and now when I read my own words, I think of how childhood impresses with its scents and lights and colors, and how childhood impresses with its absence, and how all I have of Uncle Lloyd is what began with paper.

I was ten when he died—a heart attack. Afterward, Aunt Ann wasn't well, and when she died a few years later, my father, willed the famous mural of the famous buildings, had it hung on the long wall at the office where he worked. My mother took a handful of Boehm porcelain home, perhaps two smoky gray vases. There were rumors of diamonds hidden in the Tarrytown rafters, left there to the new owners, and I don't know what happened to Candy or the bright, bright lights of the dining room. In time, I went to a university where I studied the history of science, the history of medicine, the history of cities, and when I got done, I went to work for an architect. I wanted to be near the rolled drawings, the yellow trace, the triangles and the pencils. I wanted to know the words I should have known when Uncle Lloyd was alive: *entablature, quoin, chamfer, transom, buttress, cantilever, bracket, superstructure.* I wanted genius, and obsession, and thought that I'd find both in an architect's world.

Shortly after that, a man named Joseph Caponnetto visited my parents' house with a carousel of slides and a proposition, a desire, as he later wrote in a letter to my father, "to convey some of the wonderful character of the man and his work" and "to put LM on the map as he very well should be." Caponnetto, an architect who had worked with Uncle Lloyd, who had spoken with him, who had exhausted all the available research, came with half a story told, hoping that somewhere in us, somehow among us, we would have a story to return.

We had little to give. We were ashamed (I felt ashamed) by the paucity of our memories, by the dreams we couldn't imagine, by the ways in which, each time we stretched toward truth, we were, in fact, stretching toward fiction. We were ashamed (I felt ashamed) by our utter lack of substantiating paper. Letters. Drawings. Proof of the mind of the man who had vanished.

When my father left his job in the building with the long wall, *Buildings Designed by Schultze and Weaver, Architects, from 1921 to 1936* came to live at my parents' home, in the basement, on the only wall long enough to house its expanse. The air was humid there. The mahogany sky blackened. The reflective pool went swampy. The windows and the doors of the painted buildings began to crackle and to shut, and whenever I would go home, I would visit the great mural and worry over how its gleam was rubbing off. I would show my husband—an architect I had found at the firm that employed me, an architect of delineating elegance and yellow trace and transparent triangles with a Yale education, an architect who told his stories best through line and color on every kind of paper, and who, even when he was sitting right there beside you, right there across from you, had a vanishing talent—what my Uncle Lloyd had done and tell him all that I did not know and what I couldn't remember.

And then, my mother passed away. And then, I was holding in my hands *The Journal of Decorative and Propaganda Arts*. Then, I was on page of 14 of Dolkart's contribution when, beneath a photograph of the famous mural, I found these words: "Lloyd Morgan, *Buildings Designed by Schultze and Weaver, Architects, from 1921 to 1936*, photograph of a lost oil painting, 1936. The Wolfsonian-Florida International University, Miami Beach, Florida, the Mitchell Wolfson Jr. Collection. WFIU-147. From left to right, the Hotel Pierre, the Waldorf-Astoria Hotel, and the Sherry-Netherland Hotel."

Photograph of a lost oil painting. But it wasn't lost. It was hanging in my father's basement.

My father had the painting repaired. He had it restored by two expert women who worked in a leafy neighborhood in an unfancy garage—the painting held up on mason stones and brushed and tinted back into life. I would give the process its proper cliché, *painstaking*, except that every time we visited, those restorers seemed so happy; they stopped mid-stroke to show us something new they'd found in the newly unobscured inches. Not painstaking, it seemed, at all, this unburying, this uncovering, this getting to the facts of the matter. When they were done, a truck conveyed the painting south, all the way to the Wolfsonian Museum, where there were more of Uncle Lloyd's famous drawings and a wall bright and long enough.

Not long ago, a Wolfsonian curator got in touch. She was at work on a book about the museum collections, she said, and she was hoping for more information about the un-lost painting and the man who'd made it. In preparation for a conversation, my brother rooted through a box he'd recently acquired from my father's house—a box of Uncle Lloyd memorabilia that had, before my father's most recent move, remained, at my father's request, untouched. There, in that box, was something I did not know we had—the early pages of Caponnetto's unfinished book about the man, my Uncle Lloyd, about whom too little seemed known. Typewritten and mostly double-spaced, with only occasional errors, the thirty-seven pages drew—and here, the cliché works—back the curtains:

> When he was just a lad of 10, his Father taught him the rudiments of drawing.
>
> At this time Lloyd Morgan had been taking voice lessons from Frank LaForge who was anxious for him to continue as he possessed a fine voice of wide range.

Somehow he had a great belief in night work and because of his keen interest in his work he would return to School at night while the cleaning crew did their work and when they left and put out the lights, he would continue working by candle light.

Then came the War. . . . He was machine gunned . . . by two bullets through his leg and managed to crawl back, getting a dose of gas.

While employed at Schultze and Weaver's he served as Professor at Yale University 1926–27 handling graduate students. . . . It has been said by some of the Yale students that Lloyd Morgan could, with only a mop and dirty water, present a masterpiece in rendering.

In November of 1927 [after he resigned from Yale] his office was besieged by the student body who worked under him. They arrived en masse to present to him a scroll signed by the class of 1928–1929 which describes Lloyd Morgan perfectly. It reads "To Mr. Lloyd Morgan: WE, members of Yale School of Architecture, wish to express our appreciation of the privilege of working under you last year. Your Mastery of your subject, your joy in your work, your unstinted giving of yourself for our advancement, all were an inspiration. You are not forgotten. Be assured that where your work may take you, you carry our sincerest wishes for your success."

For this fat "plum," [the Waldorf-Astoria], Leonard Schultze, an enthusiastic excitable craftsman, given to immense Corona cigars, chose Lloyd Morgan to design this structure. Only the partners and the secretary of the firm knew what it was and where it was to be erected. Lloyd Morgan isolated

> himself and created this building, working with charcoal and Wolff pencil most assiduously, day and night until he himself was satisfied with the design. Near the completion of his presentation perspective Lloyd Morgan developed an infected arm, and of course it was his right arm, caused by leaning on a thumbtack. It was Leonard Schultze who became alarmed as the arm began to fester and insisted on him visiting his doctor. The arm was lanced and Lloyd Morgan returned to the office wearing it in a sling.

As I write this, my husband is outside, charcoaling images that he will never (I've learned not to ask him) explain. I study the scans of the photos my brother also found in the box—my Uncle Lloyd's elegant face, my Aunt Ann's determined one. I try to remember one actual word my Uncle Lloyd might have said to me, one moment when he might have really seen me, when I might have been interesting enough to the man who was so perpetually interesting to me that straight out of college I took a job at an architecture firm so that I might find a partner for my life who would plan our life with paper.

A sketch.

A sweep of cartoons.

He was British-born. Philosophy, astronomy, chemistry, optics, photography somehow snagged him, resolved in him, became his legacy.

Then, there was the matter of what we now call the *blueprint*, which frankly confounded Sir John Frederick William Herschel back in the 1840s. The fact, according to Jonathan Keats in *Scientific American*, was that Herschel was in pursuit of a new photographic invention—color photography—when he began to experiment with paper he had doused with "ferrocyanate of potash," plus a touch of ammonia. Treat the paper. Leave it in the sun. Watch what happens.

What happens is blue. A permanent hue, a "cyanotype," in Herschel's made-up lexicon. But who wants a weird blue-ified photograph when you can have a far more stately black and white, for we are not extraterrestrials? No one, when the deflated Herschel was alive, could think of any good use for his cyanotype.

But just a few years after Herschel's death, at Philadelphia's Centennial Exhibition, there the cyanotype was, all decked out for a brand-new purpose that had been divined for it by a Paris firm. (Also a brand-new name: "ferro-prussiate paper.") For Herschel's bluing process, refined, was proving to be exceedingly useful to those charged with the reproduction of architectural plans. In Keats's words: "All that was required was a drawing traced on translucent paper. Pressed against a second sheet coated with Herschel's chemical under glass, the drawing was exposed to sunlight, then washed in water. The blueprint paper recorded the drawing in reverse, black lines appearing white against a cyan background."

The technology became so commonplace that, by 1926, David McKay Company, a Philadelphia publisher that had gained notoriety for publishing Shakespeare's works and would later become famous for its line of comic books, including *Popeye*, was busy touting its new release, *How to Read Blueprints*, by one W. S. Lowndes. Chapter by chapter, Lowndes cedes his blueprint knowledge—what a blueprint is, how a blueprint is used, how a blueprint is to be read, the what of a blueprint: "Whenever a dimension is given on drawings, it should be followed in preference to a scaled measurement, as the drawing may have been made out of proportion, or the paper may have either stretched or shrunk."

My great-uncle Lloyd was a blueprint guy. My husband, when I met him in the architectural offices of my first postcollege employer, worked with whiteprints, a printing technology that relies on the innate properties of diazonium salt. Now, even as our homes and opera houses and bridges and Google palaces are dreamed to life through the tap and scroll of keyboards, the bytes of lines and symbols and keys, great rolls of paper are still unfurled at building sites, and mostly, no matter the actual print technology, we call these great furls *blueprints*. We remember the sun, and how it forged them.

Instructions

Are you a collector of Shirley Temple mementos, depression glass, Elvis Presley items, or Golden Oak furniture? Then perhaps you are among the thousands of Americans suffering from "flea market fever." Attending a market can be an exhilarating experience. Seasoned shoppers have been trained to expect the unexpected; both beginning and advanced collectors are usually intent on bagging a bargain.

—Dan D'Imperio, *Flea Market Treasure*

In a slouch of loose books on a flea-market day, a title is a signature—ink so blue it might be black, letters so perfectly made that they seem to ride an invisible line. Just a name. No subtitle.

Helen Eagle.

A handmade book. An autobiography. That period at the end is hers.

In the glare of winter sun, I turn to cast a blue shadow across Helen Eagle's pages. They are thick, slick, and uniformly aged. They run twice as long as they run high, are bound by a pamphlet-stitched vermillion thread, present their contents with accurate pride. Tweed, muslin, chiffon. Rectangle, trapezoid, square. Basting, backstitch, French seam, briar stitch, buttonholes that are button-garnished, thin blue stripes impeccably patched. A drawstring pucker. An elocution of hems, one of them false.

Exculpatory captions written in the author's blue-black, well-made slant.

"Now that," the proprietor says, behind my back, "is really something."

Thirty-five dollars. I buy Helen Eagle's book for $35. I am not a seasoned shopper. I do not know what to call this volumetric artifact in which the thread, the glue, the stitches hold, this previously unimagined treasure for which I paid $33 more than every other thing I carried home from the winter flea market where the air was lemon-colored until I turned and made the shadows blue. Shut the door. *Helen Eagle.* is now mine.

Dan D'Imperio was my uncle. Victorian antiques expert. Country antiques expert. Writer of a nationally syndicated column, "Flea Market Finds." Out in the world, he scouted Lenci dolls, Schlegelmilch porcelains, Barney Google toys, and bisque nodders. In my world, he loved me best. I was his Betty Boop, the middle daughter of his only sister, who wanted to grow up to be a writer. He bought his most ridiculous gifts for me. He rolled the cuffs of his trousers and walked the littoral with me. He told me Judy Garland stories, sent me Lana Turner postcards, gossiped about film stars. He died the day before Thanksgiving, and when the phone call came, one day later, my mother took it. We had just sat down to eat. An overflowing table. We understood from my mother's face, her words, her gesture toward the steaming gravy boat that the crying would come later, after the meal was done, after we were each alone to privately reckon or never reckon with the magnitude of this loss. Loss like a secret. Loss like always.

Dear B: Having you for a niece rates as one of the best finds of my life. I am so proud to have you call me Uncle. Hope you love this book, like I love you! Uncle Dan.

There is no dedication in Helen Eagle's book. Instead, to the inside cover has been glued a folded sheet of typed instructions. This is the narrative. This is the known history, the intersection between artifact and conjecture, the means by which I imagine Helen Eagle standing on a slightly raised platform in a slightly humid classroom, the heads of the girls before her bent toward their work, her own dark curls falling loose from a ribbon. The chalkboard behind her is neat with her invisibly lined script. The air beyond the school is thick with locomotive rumble; the transport in or out of coal, metal, rubber; the talk of Teddy Roosevelt's Bull Moose Party, and now Helen Eagle remembers her place in this time on this day and looks out upon the girls who must learn sewing and begins, which is, it is true, really something:

Public Schools, Reading, Pa.

1912

SEWING

General Directions

I. Pupils should sit well back in the chair with heads erect and both feet resting on the floor, the elbows should be held at the sides of the body, and the hands in such a position that the work will be at the proper distance from the eyes.

II. Do not fasten the work to the desk or knee.

III. Never sew without a thimble. Either the top or the side of a thimble can be used.

IV. When scissors are not used, to break the thread place the left thumb-nail firmly over the last stitches; wind the thread around the right forefinger, and break the thread with the right thumb-nail. The practice of biting threads should never been allowed, both because it soils the work and it may injure the teeth irreparably.

At the funeral home, a man as tall as my uncle, with hair that frothed like my uncle's, wearing a suit and a tie that was my uncle's, introduced himself as the lover of my uncle. Thirty years, he said. Thirty years, they'd been together, the entire stretch of my life, all of it, thirty years when sometimes the lover would watch from a distance as my uncle walked the shore with me, as my uncle bought me fudge, as he sat with his sister and her entire family in a restaurant with glass windows. Does not being trusted with your favorite person's secret make love half a love, make love a question?

V. Needles must be straight and sharp and of suitable size for the fabric and thread employed.

VI. Thread should be no longer than the arm of the pupil that it may be drawn comfortably with one outer motion.

There was the funeral. There was the burial. There was an Italian lunch in a plastic-grapes-hanging-from-the-ceiling restaurant, family elbow to suffocating elbow, my mother dazed and stoic, and somewhere between the passing of the menu and the clatter of the salad, I excused myself so that I might lie on the dirty tiles of the restaurant's bathroom floor, heaving with migraine, so hot, so very cold.

Someone came to the bathroom door. Someone said it was over now, and we were going home.

I couldn't lift my head. I lifted my head.

X. Do all sewing nicely making the stitches small and even, having the wrong side look as neat as possible, and sewing the corners with great care.

XI. When obliged to take out the stitches, use the eye of a needle, and pick out one stitch at a time.

Helen Eagle's autobiography is a plain sewing sampler. Her stitches are straight.

My uncle's autobiography is "the perfect pocket reference to take along on all your flea market excursions." His more than 250 entries are alphabetically arranged.

Helen Eagle's script slants fine. My uncle's script is a garden full of poppies—the letters puffy and exuberant, the bottoms of *p*s and *j*s and *g*s dragging across the tops of *t*s and *w*s and *o*s in the line below.

Helen Eagle's hair curls at her neck as she watches her straight-backed, thimble-fingered girls hemming and patching and backstitching. My uncle's hair froths as he watches me, the one he loves best, or I thought that he did, I thought that I knew this, I thought that he loved me so thoroughly that he would trust me with his secrets.

Artifact.

Conjecture.

XIII. At the close of the lesson, the work should be carefully folded and placed in a paper envelope or pasted in a book marked with the pupil's name, which should be brought out at the next exercise.

Family Trees

She had her charms; she had her pretty. She had her choice of men, and she chose Horace, who had, as a boy, read *Robinson Crusoe* until he had become the character—stowing away in his imagination, hoarding imaginary seamen's chests, outdaring imaginary dares. *Never any young adventurer's misfortunes, I believe, began sooner, or continued longer than mine.*

A silent stranger, it was said of Horace. Brilliant, educated, a bibliophile soon enough employed by the St. Louis Mercantile Library as its director, where he would bring an innovative genius to the management of the shelves. Respected. Handsome. One eye blue and the other eye brown. The father of what would become six children, and for a while, things were fine. But children run and laugh and play and shout. Noise can press against a father's thoughts, interfere with his obsessions, and beyond the growing city of St. Louis, beyond the expanding library stacks, Horace began to retreat to the appeasing wilderness. He wrote about those woods. He wavered as library director. Increasingly, he drank. In 1903, his family by now taking refuge with Laura's kin in Ithaca, New York, and the library board demanding his resignation, Horace took a room in a St. Louis boardinghouse to keep his writing up. During a 1904 camping trip embarked on with friends, he awoke one night in a fit of shouting paranoia. The next night, back at his boardinghouse, another terrible delusion set in. The following morning, he delivered a suicide note to the bartender of Marre's Saloon and headed off to Eads Bridge to follow through on his intent.

He was arrested. He was hospitalized. He was headlines. He sought recovery in Ohio, under his father's watch. And then, in 1904, at the age of forty-two, Horace boarded a train headed south, to western North Carolina. He alighted, his *Crusoe* in hand, and walked deep into the wilderness until, in an abandoned copper-mine cabin, he set up camp. There, in that quiet, in those woods, in the company of bears and birds and crawfish, the people he chose to hunt with, fish with, study, he would grow more famous—a dean of American camping, an author of still-in-print books, a local politician, an effective proponent, along with his friend, the Japanese photographer George Masa, of the creation of the Great Smoky Mountains National Park. He'd become a man so essential in that part of the world that his name now sits upon a mountaintop.

And Laura?

On a shelf in a closet in my house is a slender packet of typewritten pages that includes a reproduction of a letter written by the couple's daughter, Lucy. It is a long letter; Lucy apologizes for its length. But she needs that length, she says, to tell her mother's story, for anyone human, as Lucy puts it, must wonder about the family whom her father had seemed to leave behind.

Lucy wants it known, she writes, that her mother did not lose her love for the man she married, that she would not abide town gossip, that anyone who made the mistake of criticizing Horace would be met with fierce rebuttals. But Lucy wants it known, too, who her mother was, how her mother had lived, what her mother might deserve in the wake of her husband's sudden death in 1931, in a car accident in that part of the world he had claimed for himself.

Lucy wants—I read the letter this way, I have read it many times—the private story of her mother to matter at least as much as the public story of her father. And why not? Why should the fame of any one eclipse the sacrifice of any other? Why aren't private lives *the* stories that matter? Why aren't those who stay behind acknowledged just as much as those who are enabled to step forward?

Because while Horace found solace in the wooded, creek-glistened south, while Horace lived his obsessions, Laura, in Ithaca, New York, rented a city house and took boarders in. On Saturdays, she did the laundry. On Sundays, she did the ironing. Five nights a week, she taught dancers to dance. In the after hour, for some extra cash, she played pretty music on the piano.

But that wasn't enough, so she took in sewing of both the plain and fancy kind. But that wasn't enough, so she baked cookies and potato chips and set them out for sale. But that wasn't enough, so she dressed other women's hair, and took care of other people's kids, and became a filing clerk. But that wasn't enough, so she wore other people's mended clothes, and her children wore other people's mended clothes, and they all looked away when the gloating townsfolk decided their poverty was worth mockery. Or gossip.

Look at Laura, wearing a neighbor's dress.

Look at Laura's children, wearing whatever almost fit.

Look at Laura, believing in the man who had left her, one supposes, with the hope that she might wash and steam and stitch and sew and give music to a dance to keep their family whole.

On good nights, Laura slept for four hours so that she might wake early to raise her children, to encourage them in their studies, to prepare them so that they might go to college, became their own somebodies. Here's the thing: They did. This includes my grandfather, George, a forester, whose second son became my father, who was baptized with the name of Horace.

My father Horace looked like his grandfather Horace. I inherited that same look—carrying forward the chiseled face, the eyes that achieved the compromise of green. I carry the known facts and the suggested myths, the pride in a name that consecrates a mountaintop, the deep appreciation for a Great Smoky Mountain vision that resulted in a national park.

But it's Laura I keep thinking of. Laura, whose eyes were I don't know what color. Laura, who had no solitary hours beside a whispering creek and managed noise in a crowded house and sought out deeply *honest* work, as Lucy, her letter biographer, writes. Laura, whose few requests at the time of her husband's death included the wish that she be given his tattered copy of his boyhood book.

Crusoe.

Because he had read that story to their children once. Because she remembered, still, that despite all else, he was capable of love.

We grow our histories into legends, into myths. We carry our genealogies forward, our faces, our answers whenever anybody asks—are you related to *that* man?

We tell the stories when we're asked, but we wonder in our silence about the wants that possess us, the bargains we make, our negotiations with the selfless and the selfish, the inescapability of our obsessions.

"The stories we tell ourselves about our ancestors have the power to shape us, in some ways nearly as much as our genetics do," Maud Newton reminds us in *Ancestor Trouble: A Reckoning and a Reconciliation.* "Many of these stories are ones we know well, while others are sublimated—hard to identify, much less articulate, more pattern-based than conscious. They can expand our sense of possibility, but they can also confine us. . . . How we imagine our ancestors, and ourselves in relation to them, can have a powerful effect on the way we live. If our lives have been circumscribed because of the way we've viewed our family, confronting our ancestors as complicated human beings rather than distant archetypes can suggest different ways of being ourselves."

Rare Books

In the aftermath of my father's death, I wanted only quiet. I chased sanctuary through shadows. I walked the vanishing miles. I lay awake in the midnight hours, but even then, a nearby fox would call out for love, or a deer would high-step through fallen leaves, or a squirrel would bumble in the gutter.

I didn't mind the birds of dawn, but I minded the eradications of tree surgeons—the carburetor rage of their chainsaws, the thonk of severed limbs hitting the ground. I minded the boot of the boy who smashed the trash bins until they crashed—spilling a bell choir of bottles. I minded the neighborhood girls' pissing accusations—*You're such a thief, you're such a liar, you stole my phone, you're such a liar.* I minded the keel of the news and the yawp of the sun. I minded the pretension of narrative, words upon words—how, even when no one was near or no one was speaking, there was a terrible howl at my ear. Worse than consonants. Louder than vowels.

I had been reading Virginia Woolf before my father died, before I rushed to him as his final storm set in, the despair of his lungs in their drowning. Turning her pages. I had been reading Virginia, also Leonard. The long swaying arms of the searchlights over their street called Paradise, in their England, 1917. The clattering machinery of the German Gotha bombers and the ascending cries of the sirens and the putter of the Royal Naval Air Service squadrons and the puff-pop of the smoke where the bombs had succeeded. A letter, sent by Virginia, to her friend Violet Dickinson, bearing news: She and Leonard have bought a table-top letterpress from the Excelsior Printing Supply Co. They are about to hand-build books of their own. Manage the text, command the art, tighten the bindings. Although the letterpress is broken when it arrives, and there are but a scant sixteen pages of how-to's to get them through the early days. They eye the letters in reverse (Caslon), take the quoin and composing stick into their hands, and decide: Virginia will set the type and bind the pages, Leonard will ink and pull. It will unfold in the dining room of the house where they live, a place called Hogarth.

Play, Leonard will one day say of the thing, *sufficiently absorbing.* Calming the noises inside Virginia's head.

Type in her composing stick.

Ink on her fingers.

A thin red thread in the eye of her needle.

Punch.

Sew.

Salvation.

In the aftermath of my father's death, I bought paper, thread, acrylic paints. Needles, brayers, buttons. Instructions I discovered I could not follow on the form and beautification of blank journals. I awled and bone folded. Knotted and snipped. I made my mistakes at the kitchen table and beside the sink, beneath bare bulbs and in swaths of sun, in the early mornings when I would wake to the fox that lived by the shatter of the moon and was bereft with love. I was not setting lines, not administering hyphens, not placing Caslon between margins. Still, I was sufficiently absorbed: color, paper, knots; ghost prints and ephemera. There was stain on my clothes and waxed linen in my needles. My hands were cracked and raw.

When story returns after story quits, it arrives in fits and fragments, rushes west, flusters east, is soft, invincible fury. I punched and patterned, tore and blended, stole flowers from the garden to preserve them. Is it like this, then, or could this be true—the hands matriculating the rage, arting the heart, deposing meaning?

Fractions arranged.

Thread kettled.

Red approximating blue.

Salvation.

An amateur obsessive.

Before my father died, when he already wasn't well, I grew frustrated with Virginia. I was reading her fiction by then, her *To the Lighthouse*. I'd sit in my bed, early in the day, and hear myself yak back at her—cut the vines of her sentences, her looping plentitudes, her times passing. I'd find an easier novel and abandon Virginia, and then I would return. Float into her sea and ride: billows and breakers, tide and tug, the nether and the offing. I'd yield. It was the only way I knew to read Virginia, although sometimes, whirlpooled into the length of a single Virginia sentence, I'd find that I was drowning. That I could not understand Virginia.

And yet: On the eve of COVID-19, my father older than he'd ever been, my father in the early phase of passing, I went to the Kislak to visit Virginia. To hold what she'd made with her hands in my hands. To reckon with what remains when those we battle with, and love, go missing. I'd wait inside that clean box of that reading room for Virginia's letterpress work to be retrieved. At a long table before an assembly of soft supports that hold the archived and retrieved in a non-spine-breaking *V*, she came.

Her thick and desiccated pages.

Her assertions of ink.

Her chipped and fraying bindings.

Her nether and her offing.

I held what she'd made with her hands in my hands. I pretended permanence.

We go to books for solace, and for proof, to begin again at the beginning. Handmade books, first editions, inky manuscripts, especially. They carry time forward on their own electric currents. They keep what we can't keep. They counterweight the dying.

Thumbprints.

Center knots.

Errors.

That crease in the top corner.

The infuriating riddle.

Hold the old book in your hand, and you are holding something living.

When the famed Philadelphia bibliophile A. S. W. Rosenbach (1876–1952) was eleven years old, he bought, for the grand sum of $24, an illustrated copy of *Reynard the Fox*. Young Rosenbach didn't have the necessary cash on hand, but he had the support of a book-obsessed uncle, in whose shop on Commerce Street the boy had been working since the age of nine. A deal was struck. A book was won.

In "Talking of Old Books," reprinted in *Books and Bidders: The Adventures of a Bibliophile*, Rosenbach remembers the early undertow of what would become his lifelong obsession:

> *At that age I could hardly realize, spellbound as I was, the full quality of mystery and intangible beauty which becomes a part of the atmosphere wherever books are brought together; for here was something that called to me each afternoon, just as the wharves, the water, and the ships drew other boys who were delighted to get away from books the moment school was out.*

Rosenbach was, in the words of Vincent Starrett, a writer for the *Chicago Tribune*, "an excellent bibliografer, something of a scholar, and a bookman who would have lived by books, for books, and with books whatever his station in life might have been. It was his initial love and knowledge of old books that made it possible for him to become the great figure known as 'the Doctor' in the auction rooms of Europe and America."

And what a figure Rosenbach cut—a University of Pennsylvania graduate with a Ph.D. in English literature, whose book-acquiring adventures were often front-page news. Over the course of a life that never swerved from rare books, he held the manuscripts of Chaucer, Lewis Carroll, and James Joyce in his hands (not to mention a considerable number of Gutenberg bibles, the copy of *Moby-Dick* that Herman Melville presented to Nathaniel Hawthorne, and a letter from Cervantes); amassed a fortune in children's books (most of them donated, toward the end of his life, to the Free Library of Philadelphia); fed the bookish appetites of such men as Pierpont Morgan and Henry Folger; named his fishing boat *First Folio*; wondered why no wife of a U.S. president had become a genuine book collector; and "made it a rule," as he writes in *A Book Hunter's Holiday*, "to look at any book which is directed my way." His final Philadelphia residence, in the twentieth block of Delancey Street, is now the home of the Philip H. and A. S. W. Rosenbach Museum and Library, and it is here where book lovers can, by appointment, see some of the books, letters, and manuscripts Rosenbach could never quite part with himself.

Dard Hunter, in his dusty shoes and hat, his workman's shirt and tucked tie, traveled the world in search of not just paper but rare books written by other paper lovers. Rosenbach—cigar smoke rising, whiskey swirling, millionaires waiting—dominated auction rooms. They were men of their times, bound by the thrill of the chase and the deep reprieve of history and the hope for the eternal.

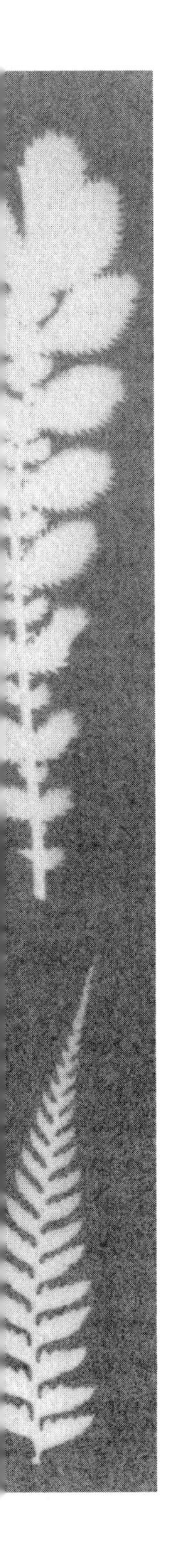

Possession

Dear Dard:

How is it that in all this time of writing you, my laptop refuses the concession—autocorrecting your name every chance it gets, so that you become Dare and Hard and Dart and Dad—*Dad*, Dard, *Dad*—but never (until I force the fix) Dard? As if our technology cannot make room for the ephemeral. As if you are to be standardized. As if only your conventional, utterly forgettable baptized name will do: William Joseph. A name not nearly as fitting as Dard, which you acquired at a young age (legend has it) when you, pointing toward your beloved big brother, could only say *Dard*, and not *Darling*.

Adorable, isn't it? Why don't we call him Dard*?*

Your name as your original possession.

I'm offended for you, Dard. I'm offended on behalf of you, your son, and your grandson, your succession of namesakes. I'm offended, let's be blunt, that your name resounds only in the smallest of circles, that when I speak of you, I mostly have to explain you, list out your achievements, tell a proving tale or two.

You were an introvert and an occasional fame-quester.

You were a rotten businessman.

You were poor, but you were rich.

Your only talents in the kitchen were a bowl of cereal and a splash of milk.

You doubted, in the end, yourself: *If I have done anything spectacular. . . .*

But you knew that the collected possessions of your endless journeys were material. You thought that you might build yourself your own museum, there at Lime Rock, among the ghosts of the old foundry, but that didn't happen. You ceded, after a tussle, to the beckoning hand of Karl Compton, the president of the Massachusetts Institute of Technology (MIT), who in 1938 offered your thousands of items a campus home. Books, paper molds, watermarks, manuscripts, documents, wood blocks, tapa, Dard II says (the list is his). Wooden crates and fireproof safes.

As if all that you owned was all that you were.

It took you and your oldest son six months to unpack and display the things of your life, but this museum, officially launched in 1939, didn't make you happy. You weren't, your son says, "at ease." You expressed, in a letter to your friend Elmer Adler, a terrible sense of being out of place on a campus where science and technology was all full-speed ahead and the past was minor, slight, a historical inconvenience. You wanted to place what you loved among people who would get it, and so in 1954, you were at last released by MIT to move your museum to the Institute of Paper Chemistry in Appleton, Wisconsin, where Arnold Grummer was becoming legend. You'd been dead for two decades when the museum moved again, to Atlanta, Georgia, so that now the stuff of your life, or the stuff your grandson does not himself proudly preserve and share, lives in the Robert C. Williams Museum of Papermaking, and there, as part of Georgia Tech's Renewable Bioproducts Institute, it is destined to remain.

Permanent, Dard. *Permanently* ensconced.

Your material as your measure.

Your name spoken by the schoolchildren who visit, the scout troops, the Georgia Tech students, the papermakers and paper artists and paper historians, the members of the North American Hand Papermakers, the curious-minded, the idle wanderers who find themselves on the northern edge of that ingenious campus, open the doors, and stay. The stuff of your life is haloed there, backlit, placarded. The story of paper is the story as you might have told it—a story of intuition, experimentation, and surprise; insights shared, stolen, whispered, bound; machines that slice and stamp and soak and press; a woman wearing pearls and buckles on her shoes as she cuts the rags. It's molds and deckles, watermarks and manuscripts, photographs and captions, stories hanging on by their fibrous threads.

The tracery of your obsession, preserved by your possessions.

My husband and I traveled some eight hundred miles to find you here, which is not your million miles, but still. We spent the night in a club hotel on the edge of Centennial Olympic Park, beside a giant Ferris wheel. We waited for the sun and then walked the red-brick park (here: the aquarium; there: the Coke museum; somewhere: the quilts of origins and remembrance and dreams; always and subconsciously: the crescendo and vanish of fountain water sprays), and then a road named Luckie, reaching the southern boundary of the college campus and skirting its edge. I hauled my heavy camera, which I would never use, and a decent pair of shoes. My husband navigated our progress with his phone. It was a weekday, October, school in session, but when we finally cut into the Georgia Tech campus and made our way among the many geometries and the slant shade of the tall evergreens, our encounters with students, teachers, other wayfarers were rare.

Approaching you in quiet, then. Approaching without fanfare. We opened the door, walked in. We could go right, or we could go left, so we chose left and made our way to the George Mead Education Gallery. I stood alone among the stuff of paper, one proof of history at a time:

> Until the end of the 19th century, the process of papermaking involved extraordinary searches for rags to make paper. As the demand for paper grew, the papermakers became more desperate to find rags for fibre. Zenas Crane, an early papermaker, persuaded postriders (mail carriers on horseback) to spread the news to farmers to save their rags and take them to the village stores. Papermakers and poets wrote poems and songs to influence the public to save rags. The majority of paper was made from old clothing, gunpowder sacks, and blankets.
>
> At the paper mills women placed the rags in a duster to remove the dirt, washed them, separated the cotton from the linen, and removed stained pieces, buttons and hooks. At a rag table, women sliced the rags with a long blade to produce cloth strips three to four inches wide. The strips were rolled into balls with the mineral lime and left to rot.
>
> The most experienced papermaker in the mill, and usually the owner, was a vatman. He formed the sheets of paper, dipping the mold and deckle into a large wooden or metal vat. The vat contained a mixture of 10% pulp and 90% water that had been "charged" or stirred with a long pole. The vatman dipped the mold and deckle into the mixture and lightly shook them back and forth, binding the paper fibers together. To drain excess water from the paper, he held the mold and deckle at an angle. Then the vatman passed the mold to the coucher.

My husband perpetually ahead of me, eclipsing the centuries at his personal museum-going speed, calling, *Look. Look.*

I'm reading, I wanted to say. *I'm thinking.* But those words weren't right, so I didn't say them. What I was doing was conjuring the many versions of you—the man who found the artifacts, the man who took them home, the man who dreamed of a museum one day, but never imagined Atlanta, or this supplemented display, by which I mean that here, at this museum, the gaps in your collection have been overcome. The story of paper has been completed (if only incrementally) by the gifts and words of others. A model of the first Robert papermaking machine. A heavy wooden stamper. A replica you didn't build or own of the bucolic Rittenhouse paper mill, America's first. Those cows on the green hills by the creek grazing. That waterwheel paused in its turning.

My husband left the first exhibit room, cut through the lobby, urged me to join him and see, but I took my stubborn time, for I had been waiting for so long to stand among that which had followed your if: *If I have done anything spectacular.*

All, I thought, in its good time—the Chinese methods, the early tools, the tapa and the vellum and the parchment that are not paper, your portrait, in the little room they call the shrine. *Take my picture*, I said to my husband, handing him my phone. You looked straight ahead, didn't blink. You will, Dard, never see me.

Nor will you ever know Virginia Howell, who directs this museum and opened her office door to my husband and me and the friend who joined us in the afternoon. Many of your books live now in a glass room adjacent to Virginia's office, and when I asked her to show me the volumes that intrigue her, she graciously began. Part VII of Romeyn Hough's *American Woods*, with its razor-thin slivers of trees. One of the six volumes produced by Dr. Jacob Schäffer, the eighteenth-century Bavarian who harvested the stuff of his own garden so that he might see what sort of sheets are formed by moss or asbestos or thistles, and into which you wrote, with pencil, right there across rare history, the names of ingredients: *sweet broom, fir apple, roof tiles.* A red-cloth covered catalog of Chinese postcards. Your own *Papermaking in China and Japan*, that *Litt.D.* after your name by then, thanks to an honorary degree.

And then there were the stories Virginia began to tell, about her own family roots in Chillicothe, about your Mountain House, and about your son, Dard II, who designed the wedding bands that her grandparents wore and whose very life was saved by Virginia's own great-grandmother, who whisked him away to the hospital when he was a kid with a burst appendix and a Christian Scientist for a mother, a kid who would have died without such great-grandmotherly quick thinking (and practical disregard for Edith's famous Christian Scientist stance, which she applied to the health of her own children).

"Wait," I heard myself interrupting Virginia. "Wait. Your great-grandmother? Saved Dard II's life?"

Virginia nodded, Dard, as if this were the simplest fact in the world, the most minor of coincidences. That the steward of your possessions—the woman who preserves your things and thinks progressively forward about how to inspire others to learn and love and cherish paper—comes from a family who saved your most important legacy of all. Your son, and, by the laws of genealogy, your grandson, the Dards who devoted so much of their own lives to ensuring that your name, your obsessions, your possessions live on.

Your story pulses and blinks, deletes itself and thrives. Your name is ceaselessly remade—Dark, Dad, Hard, Card—and I ceaselessly remake it. Your artifacts *speak.* They are spoken through. If we shape our theories about you according to the things you preserved, what theories will we shape about ourselves? What do the ticket stubs we never tossed out mean? The address book that has lost its proper binding? The antique library card? The receipt for last year's boots? Why do we steal our mother's paper doilies? Why do we keep the uncashed checks? What will be our final tally? Who will preserve what we thought to keep? Who will write our history? What will be our measure?

Ticket

It is April 1969, and the most beautiful show in the world is on—Shipstads & Johnson Ice Follies. Starring the incomparable Peggy Fleming, Olympic gold medalist; Ron and Cindy Kauffman, U.S. national pairs skating champions; and Mr. Frick, the skating clown with the Gumby ankles, who can squat himself down on a barrel after spread eagling rampages around it and march in time with "Seventy-Six Trombones" and avoid colliding with another clown's back end. It's superspecial and most hysterical, and my whole family's going; we have nosebleed tickets at the Boston Colosseum. We will wear our ironed clothes and bury sibling squabbles so as to command our best behavior. We will pitch far forward in our pull-down seats, and we'll know to break the fall. We will stomp our frozen feet during intermission and keep our jackets on in the chill. We will never leave unless one of us is sure that no more silver-bladed encores are hovering behind the Zamboni curtains. And when photographs of then are returned to us, the spotlights will so obliterate the stars that all we'll see is halos.

Tickets as promise.

Stubs as proof.

Ho! for the ironclad ship! The yard will be open for visitors on Friday & Saturday. The launch will take place at noon, Saturday, May 10th, 1862. Passengers can take the 2d & 3d Street passenger cars. Exchange tickets are sold by all connecting roads (1862)

Grand floral and strawberry fair for the benefit of the Union Volunteer Refreshment Saloon commencing Monday, June 16th, at the saloon, foot of Washington Street. Tickets for sale here. Also on all passenger rail-road cars. Price 10 cents (1862)

Horticultural Hall. By special request! 3 nights longer! Monday, Tuesday and Wednesday, Feb. 9, 10 & 11, prices reduced! Admission, 20 cents or 8 tickets for $1.00. Williams South Sea whaling voyage. . . . Remember—tickets are only 20 cents Eight tickets, one dollar Remember Wednesday afternoon. Evening—doors open at 7—commence at 7 3/4. Afternoon—doors open at 2—commence at 3 (1863)

Fun! Fun! Fun! The Soldiers' Ethiopian Troupe! Will be at [blank] on [blank] eve'ng [blank] '64 This troupe is composed entirely of wounded soldiers! Now is the time to serve your country's defenders. Admission, 25 cents Tickets to be had at the door. Doors open at 7 o'clock. To commence at half-past 7 (1864)

Something new! The Copperhead will be dissected by scalpel at Chamberlin's Hall, Moline, on Wednesday evening, March 30, '63 Tickets 25 cts., to be had at the door (1864)

In the Library Company of Philadelphia records, the show is always about to begin.

Library Card

I was singing "Kumbaya." Then, Bob Dylan. I was pumping harder and higher, kicking my feet through the sky, when a rusted chain on the backyard swing set snapped, and I went flying. Gravity sheared my wings. I smashed the earth with my weight.

"Mom?" I cried, more like a question. A yelp of time and the floating white of cloudscapes. Finally, she heard me, ran for me, the backdoor screen door slammed. She kneeled beside me in the dirt and scooped me up, into her arms. My father drove. She sat in the back beside me. She sat somewhere far away in the hospital while I waited, in a hallway, on a gurney, for the only doctor who could set my particular kind of a shattered arm to return from the beach, where he'd been sunning. For the next many years, I'd wear one version of a cast or another—the first to my shoulder, the next to my elbow, the others tight as short, fingerless gloves.

The point is: When contact sports were in session, gym was erased from my school schedule. I was relegated to the library. Relegated, it seemed to me at first, to the very farthest margins. Then, I emerged as someone new: a bona fide librarian's pet.

Stamping the due-date cards, thumbing the catalog cards, shelving the books on the stacks, *shh-ing* the patrons—I did my duties. By the time I reached college, I had marketable skills and a job at the Van Pelt Library. I worked circulation and shelving. I trailed book dust and stamp ink. I acquired the answers to some questions. I met a dark-bearded boy who was obsessed with Tolstoy, Dostoevsky, Gogol, Turgenev. "Look," he said, when, after months of working side by side, he took me to his apartment. "Here," he said, offering a bowl of thick pea soup. There was no place to sit, so we sat on the floor, surrounded by all the Russian novels he had stolen.

Other than that, I might have loved him.

The best of them were hard to come by. They were expensive, too. Eager for more, frustrated by constraints, Benjamin Franklin made a persuasive proposition: Why not a circulating library—a home, in other words, for books? Fifty members of his junto said yes, formalizing the agreement in the summer of 1731 and pooling the money with which they would buy the first volumes for the nation's first ("successful") lending library, the Library Company.

In 1814, the Athenaeum of Philadelphia, another member-supported institution, opened its doors with the express purpose of providing access to "general knowledge," not to mention, eventually, a happy haven for chess and an abundance of architectural records and drawings.

But it was the Free Library, chartered in 1891 by William Pepper, that made the borrowing of books a democratic pastime in the nation's birthplace. Its first iteration was a mere three rooms located in city hall, where book borrowers were each equipped with their own personalized card that was to be presented "with every book returned." The rules, as expressed right there on the card, were explicit and enforced:

> *A fine of one cent per day is charged for keeping books beyond that period; two cents additional will be charged for each notice sent by post, and if it becomes necessary to send a messenger to secure the return of the book, an additional fine of twenty-five cents shall be paid.*

No books will be delivered on cards where fines are unpaid.

The Free Library would soon move to a new home at 12th and Chestnut, and next to quarters at 13th and Locust, before finally taking up permanent residence at 1901 Vine Street, where it remains today, more than one hundred years on, harboring the relics of before and staging the voices of our times.

Receipt

The toe ring that you acquired with your Mole Hole sales clerk money. The earrings for your second pair of piercings. The books you won't have room for. The dress you'll never wear. The shoes in which you nearly sprained your ankle. The coat you could not actually afford. The sapphire you bought yourself for surviving surgery because someone had to, the flowers with which you embellished the aftermath, the carton of milk, the extra butter, the salmon and the parsley, the envelopes, the stamps, the gifts, and now paint and thread and linter; cork and cardboard and linen; upcycled leather and white sulfite, ephemera and buttons, more books you won't have room for.

The receipt as your witness: You were there in the moment of your choosing.

On December 20, 1850, Mrs. Fisher bought, among other items, one *Pathways of Lord* for $7.50 from the George S. Appleton bookseller at 164 Chestnut Street, on the corner of Seventh. On February 8, 1853, from Parkinson's Saloons of 311 Chestnut Street, the same Mrs. Fisher bought quite the assortment of BonBons, Secrets, and Ornaments. Mr. Harvey Chew, for his part, completed his $13.72 purchase of special liquor from B. Lieber of 283 Market Street, Importer of Brandies, Wines, Gins, London Porter, Scotch Ale, Absinthe, Curacoa (*sic*), &c., on a certain December day in 1852, while, on a scribbled day in 1850—December 13? August?—someone (the receipt is incomplete) was buying yards of muslin, calico, and linen for a mere $3.41 from the James S. Jones Wholesale & Retail Dealer in Fancy & Staple Dry Goods & Trimmings, Hosiery, Globes, Embroideries, Ribbons and Dress Trimmings, Cloths, Cashmeres, Vestings, Furnishing Goods, &c, a shop located on the Main Street of Germantown, opposite the Friends' Meeting House.

Receipts speak. Just consider these, held in the digital collection in the Library Company of Philadelphia. They force the imagination toward a particular city block, an arrangement of store, a rustle of conversation between the merchant and the clerk, a bundling of a parcel and a weight, a transport and a place in a kitchen, on a shelf, by a fireplace. Among plenty? Within silence? As a solace? As a cure? A receipt is desire and need. It is debt versus dream. It is hunger. It is more.

Paper Doily

I thieved her doilies. Paper. White. After she was gone, from the kitchen where she'd stood (always shoes on her feet, never in bare stockings). All those ten months, my father and I had emptied out and cleaned that house, and in the end, I found her doilies, and I stole them.

I vowed to make cakes to put on them, to fancy myself up—old-fashioned-like, domestic. To stand in my own small kitchen with my own shoes on and peel one doily from the next, slowly and carefully, as she would do, slipping a short, clean nail between the crunch of layers, then slipping the doily into platter position, in anticipation of a cake.

There is a satisfying sound to the isolation of a single doily from its compact pack, a small positive-negative thrill, as the emptiness that denotes the geometry releases itself to the air. As memory releases itself. As the little broken parts of the perforated paper fall, silent like the dust they are becoming.

In that house built on a curve and a hill she had stood, looking out on the long swoop of a driveway as she worked. Her sweet-icinged carrot cakes baked in modest tins. Her cheesecakes with graham-cracker crusts sprung from springform pans. Her layered cakes into which she'd slip waxed-papered coins. Something she called Daddy's Delight, which entailed chocolate wafers encased by stiffened whipped cream, was frozen ahead of being served, and then bias sliced.

All that time, I was the lonesome in me—my mind perpetually somewhere else, on a crest of want and wish. While she baked her cakes, while she separated her doilies, I locked myself into the basement to dance. *Hearts. Wild World. Diamond Girl.* My mind like a muscle when I danced, caught up in its twitch.

Then, her baking done, she called to me. Up the basement stairs I went. Into her kitchen, where the carpet was green and the wallpaper was mostly green and her eyes were, and there, on a doily, her new cake sat. Warm as a truce.

I steal her doilies to steal her back.

A paper doily descends from a cotton doily, which was the invention of a sixteenth-century Londoner who trafficked in textiles of the "openwork" sort. A cotton doily on a table, on a pillow, on a couch became, in time, a touch of elegance, until it distinctly was not, until the very sight of a cotton doily incited suspicions of dust, and you could buy them by the dozens for cheap in flea-market malls; nobody wanted to be caught with cotton doilies.

But my mother's paper doilies were something else. My mother's paper doilies were the cakes she still had planned, the cakes she might have baked, the cakes that would have brought me back, I was always going to go back, I had not planned to leave her, and now, today, when I am speaking to friends and I say *doilies*, all their stories come tumbling back, and there we stand, without our mothers.

Legal Tender

The time I called and could not find them. Drove to their house, and they were gone. Called their friends, and no one knew. Thought all the terror thoughts, imagined my life without them. Circled the empty with my imagination. Days later, they emerged. Casual. The story, over months, broke free. They'd criss-crossed states to buy, for another, a second car. A very secret mission.

Christmas, toward the end, was a marathon. A preponderance of packages, the names of others on the tags. I'd sit for hours in their family room and (for the sake of decency) applaud, desperate to be anywhere but there. It was all so deeply operatic—so many multitudes of encores, until afterward, when I thought the ordeal done, up from their basement would come another box, big as a crate, in which more bows bobbed. A box, my mother said, that had nearly been forgotten.

I could not stay. I could no more watch.

Secret deposits, secret transfers, secret wishes granted until I began to fight for the truth, to argue against the logic, to ask what I had done to become, in their eyes, less than.

Washingtons, Jeffersons, Lincolns, Hamiltons, Jacksons, Grants, and Franklins, checks and checkbooks, bank accounting? Does legal equal tender? Why be so myopic?

And what to do with the last parcel my father ever sent me, months before he died in COVID-era quarantine? My name and address crooked on the envelope, written with the crooked in his fingers. His address crooked on the back, crooked with his blocky letters. The envelope Scotch-taped shut, the original gum arabic still intact, the check inside written first in pink marker and then in red marker, none of the words where they belonged, the date gone missing. No note, no nothing, except for the check and its neon amount, which turned my face hot with its implied apology for all the years of being less than.

My father would not take a phone to his ear by then. I could not go to see him. I could not tell him how I had never wanted money. I had just wanted my share of their love. I'd just wanted to earn it.

Whelk. Beads. Species. Goods in exchange for other goods. And then came paper money, which, in America, made its way into circulation toward the end of the seventeenth century. It was convenient: find a press, print some money. It was confusing: Who's to say that bit of pocket stain and crumple is actual, valuable, legal tender?

It was Benjamin Franklin, a paper, type, and ink guy (among other things, Franklin financed a number of paper mills), who fought the counterfeiters with some ingenious dollar-printing tricks—including an intricate depiction of an intricate leaf. But more than his singular ingenuity was required to fight the British who tried to stamp out America's inconvenient paper money; indeed, the Stamp Act of 1765 was designed to heavily tax all paper goods at a time when the demand for paper was far outpacing the supply.

The British, in the end, didn't win, and ragpicking became the province of the nineteenth-century poor, with children taught to hunt old rags down and sell them to the local paper mills, whose paper would, in part, feed the currency machine. Rags to riches, the story went, a phrase both literal and metaphorical, as Jonathan Senchyne notes in "Rags Make Paper, Paper Makes Money: Material Texts and Metaphors of Capital": "In the Delaware River Valley, a major regional center of nineteenth-century papermaking, schoolteachers took children on field trips to paper mills. Often these stories and lessons were meant to encourage household economy in children, while also teaching them about the industrial landscape surrounding them."

Think of it: the dirty clothes becoming the pulp becoming the value. Think of the stuff itself: the frayed, the torn, the stained, the overworn, anything a waterwheeled machine might macerate, anything that might be molded. Think of those kids, being instructed. What does it mean, then, money? What is it finally worth? Everything and nothing, and then absolutely nothing, when your parents are now disappeared, and you can never ask them.

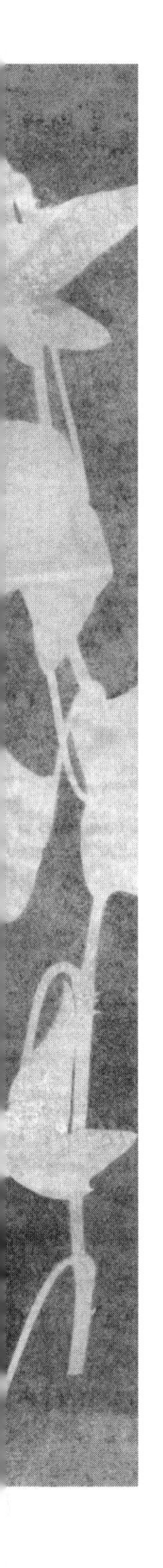

Ambition

Dear Dard:

The punchline of this story is your silence. The big smash of nothing that you say at the end. The way you won't reveal yourself as the hero of your story.

Setting the stage as you set the stage: You have been traveling for days, eight thousand miles. You are lonesome, heartsick, caught in a storm, near a quay, in New Zealand. You are feeling, in your modestly selected word, *discouraged.*

With nothing to do before your next mode of transit appears, you wake early in the morning and make your way through a slashing downpour to the Wellington Museum. Which has not yet opened. Will not open for an hour. Nothing to do, you conclude, but stand in the museum entrance, taking in the gray dispiriting sop of weather, questioning your choices, wishing you were home with Edith and the boys, in the comfort of Ohio. What had you been thinking, anyway? One more journey? One more book? All those hours on your feet, with your type, in your head, sorting, transcribing, remembering.

But now, here comes a stranger. Another lonesome somebody running through the slash of weather. He, too, will pause at the museum entrance for some respite and, in time, some conversation. The stranger is a New Zealand native. He's spent a single day, he reveals, in the United States.

Just one day? you ask.

He explains that this one-day tour of America happened two decades prior, in 1906. That he'd been part of a traveling band playing Canadian venues and that one day, for only (again) that one day, the troupe had crossed over into the United States to a village called East Aurora, where, in his words, as you quote them, "an eccentric old man with long hair, flowing black tie, and a broad-brimmed hat had a socialistic community there." The stranger in New Zealand went on to explain Elbert Hubbard to Dard, that Roycroft shop. Dard listened. The man kept talking.

Saying this:

> After our band concert was over in the village, the elderly gentleman with the long hair gave us each an inscribed book as a personal favor. My book was a story about a man who went for a nap in the Catskill Mountains and remained asleep for twenty years. I believe the writer was Irving Washington. I always liked that little book, bound in soft leather. In my untrained way I admired the peculiar decorations. On the last page of the book it was printed that the designs had been made by a person named Dard Hunter. Odd name, that. The rain's about over and I must be off. . . .

Jesus, Dard, how did you do that? How did you not lean toward the stranger and reveal yourself? How were you not tempted to conduct a minor boast, to name the vast coincidence, to startle the stranger with the news that you were none other but Dard Hunter yourself?

The Dard Hunter, who had already become, in the words of your namesake son, Dard II, "the first person in the entire history of bookmaking to have produced, by the hand method of the fifteenth century, a complete book, including the paper, type, and printing."

"An extreme individualist," your first son called you. A man who managed to be "a most modest and unpretentious person, as so often is the case with really great people." A man who

> always attempted to avoid public attention or acclaim whenever possible. In spite of four honorary degrees, three medals, and numerous positions of esteem in his field of graphic arts, bestowed on him in recognition of his faithful and untiring efforts in world-wide research in paper making and in the art of book-making, he remained unimpressed. His sole comment about these honours was, "For such a remote subject as I have chosen as a life work, it is always a wonder to me that I am recognized at all in the educational field. The title of 'Doctor' amuses me no end."

Your oldest son was in some ways like you—your Dard Hunter II, whose accomplishments as a type forger, bookmaker, furniture builder, antiquarian collector, curator, relentlessly devoted publisher of *The Life Work of Dard Hunter*, went, in the words of his son, Dard III, "largely unnoticed because of his very modest nature and the natural shadowing effect created by his father."

And Dard III? He speaks with a voice one must lean in to hear. He doesn't embarrass the obsessed woman who dares to write something new about the man who might have disdained the fluttery nature of her project, who dares to proclaim her enterprise with a nearly knock-off title. Instead, he writes with words you might have chosen: *I must confess that corresponding to someone with your creative writing abilities is akin to a carpenter holding a meaningful conversation with Einstein about the theory of relativity. Your work is impressive and the concept for your most recent book intriguing. Thank you for being inspired to include my grandfather.*

Modesty, Dard: Its power can't be dimmed. It exhilarates me and leaves me here, on the page surmounting my own pride.

Homework (Redux)

Beth Kephart
History 133
9/17/79
Mr. Dickey
"Intellectual History: Its Method and Aim"

Aside from your tendencies to "over write" and to attribute too much completeness & definiteness to what intellectual historians do, this is a lively little essay. You do, at points, misuse words, but that is a minor problem. Overall, you seem to be on solid ground. I hope the excitement you feel about intellectual history persists—judging from your writing there is a little too much "scientism" in your outlook & a dose of intellectual history will cure you of that by giving you a more flexible perspective. Any questions? Come see me.

A–/B+

Beth Kephart
Intellectual History 133
Mr. Dickey
October 16, 1979

"The Problem with Building Societies on the Foundation of Illusion"

You've obviously given this a lot of thought—and you've neatly worked the information on the Scientific Revolution into the essay. This puts your discussion of Condorcet on solid ground. Where you go wrong, I think—a missed opportunity really—is with Faust. For some reason you have chosen to identify Goethe with Faust—that posed a problem, for it makes it impossible for you to pick up the Faust material (religion warning science) and Goethe's ambivalence to the science-religious question.

B+

Beth Kephart
Professor Dickey
November 11, 1979
"Paper 1"

You still feel more comfortable with C than G. Your use of [unclear] is good; but you don't really follow up on it in your explanation of G's relative to F (i.e., G's attitude to the [unclear]).

A–

Beth Kephart
Professor Dickey
November 14, 1979
"Hegel and Motion"

I don't understand—you asked me, "When can we write about Abrams . . ." So here's a question where a careful reading of Abrams offers a payoff. And what do you do—no Abrams! This prompts me to wonder about your question selection—you're obviously working hard, doing much outside reading—but your work lacks sharpness and focus. Why? I can't put my finger on it. Perhaps you're setting your sights too high in this course. That is laudatory but often self destructive.

B

I have them here, my college papers, but I refuse to read my own essays, refuse to shame myself with the murk of my poor thinking, refuse to assiduously retrace me. What matters to me are the words written to me. How often I was warned against myself, and how poorly I kept listening.

File Folder

Manila. Tabbed. Moldering in the cement coffin of the basement. Beneath the hover of the pale, trapped bees. Inside the veil of webs. Under the crawl of stink bugs, centipedes, fighting ants. The history there, between the tabs. The words I wrote for other people. The words I helped them want to say.

These are yours. Take them. Be them.

What to do with it all—those times, passing. The years I spent leaning toward power to fortify power. The stories I was told so that I might craft them in the voices of those who wished to tell them. The torquing of pronouns—whose *I* was whose *I*, and the rule was: It didn't matter. The letters to employees: signed *X*. The letters to stockholders: signed *Y*. The speeches for the summoned: in an arena, in a boardroom, around a conference table. The books, even, with their names on them, as if the books had been there all along, in the minds of those for whom I wrote them.

In the chilled, damp cellar, they linger. The histories I textured, the ideals I glossed, the visions I slid beneath the lace of poetry, the sleights of voice and reason. I gave it all away, but there it remains: witness to my ghosthood. A thousand more years, and it will be nothing.

In "Granular Certainty, the Vertical Filing Cabinet, and the Transformation of Files," Craig Robertson tells the story of Elihu Root, a big-name lawyer who became overwhelmed by archaic governmental filing systems after stepping into the role of secretary of state in 1905, under Theodore Roosevelt.

The prevailing practice, Robertson writes, was not just archaic but static:

> *Clerks used press books or copybooks to store incoming and outgoing correspondence in separate, chronologically ordered, bound volumes with limited indexing. The tipping point for Root came when a request for a handful of letters resulted in several large bound volumes appearing on his desk. In response, he demanded that a vertical filing system be adopted. In 1906, the department began to use a numerical subject-based filing system housed in vertical filing cabinets; a more comprehensive decimal filing system followed in 1910.*

Root was, by no means, the inventor of such a system; people had for years been organizing their unbound paper in a variety of drawers, nooks, and crannies, and in a preponderance of ways. But by favoring the separation of thematically aligned papers into loose files, as opposed to bound books, Root was one of many who laid the foundation for the manila folders that own our histories today—those standardized, tabbed, heavy-duty thought-and-history containers.

Those proofs of the hours we spent, the glory, or the shame, accumulated.

Robertson's article is rich with colorful visuals (some drawn from the author's own manila folder collection). It charms with efficient authority. And it is worth quoting at length, for it is Dard-like, I think, with its emphasis on weights and grains and fibers. I'll never look at my own tabbed history in quite the same way, having read these words by the vertical file scholar:

The industry quickly coalesced around folders made out of a single sheet of manilla paper. The use of a specific kind of hemp rather than wood pulp made this paper thicker. Known as "Manila Hemp," abaca fibre came from a species of banana unique to the Philippines and had arrived on the northeast of the U.S. care of "grass rope" on Filipino ships; a patent for manila paper was issued in 1843. When used in the manufacturing of folders, manila paper was folded once, so the front flap was approximately one-half inch shorter than the back to create a space to label the contents of the folder. It was accepted that to support the weight of its contents when being taken out of a drawer, the paper needed to be folded so that the paper's fibres or grain ran from top to bottom but not side to side.

Dictionary

A gift, but from whom? My mother? Would she have wanted this for me—more words? In the marrow of my imagination, on the pages of my stories, in the gutter in between our lives? Here, for you, these words.

Dudgeon.

Umbrage.

Miff.

My husband? Straining through remembering to see it, I can't see it. Although his arms are strong, and it would have been easy for him to carry so many words. To haul them around. To leave them for me so that he could leave them behind. What use has he ever had for words?

A through M.

N through Z.

Me, then. I gave myself these *on historical principles* words, these seven-point-five million words, these thirteen-point-five pounds of words, this 1993 edition. The liquids and the nasals. The † preceding the obsoletes, the ***bold italics*** shouting *foreign*, the vowel diagrams representing *the position and degree of raising the tongue in articulating the sound*, the birth dates and the bells tolled for words, and then—inevitable?—the crash of them to the floor from the shelves in the black business of the night.

In the pool of morning sun, they were a devastated splay of words.

I picked them up. I adjusted their spines. I straightened their jackets, their slick and now permanently battered outerwear. I smoothed the mess within, the small crests rippling the pages, so thin. I put it all to rest—A through M and N through Z—in one corner of the floor, stacking the volumes on their sides, so that they became a two-story house of words with thumb-index windows, six inches tall, three inches per story. Spiders moved in with their web filigrees. Breezes riffled overhead. Dust grayed the gloss. Time took its time in the house of words.

Across the room from the house of words, I tapped my keyboard, searched my screen. I hunted my plosives, fricatives, and affricates with digital passivity. My differentiated homonyms. My variant spellings. No heavy lift required. No crouching in the shadows. No splitting of index-finger skin on the thin, thin pages of the *Shorter Oxford*. The words I found and used were immaterial. They were tap and dot and vapor words.

Antinomy.

Inconstant.

Squander.

It must have been my gift to myself. It could not have been my mother. Straining through remembering to see it, I see it. See me in a velvet gown. (Aubergine.) See me on a night when I have been noticed for my words. At the door to the ceremony, I wait. *I will be there*, my mother has said. She does not come, she never comes, I'm waiting.

Heartsore.

Cureless.

Brume.

In time, it was as if there were no words in the house of words. As if the house of words had become a construction, a kind of furniture, those six inches tall, those nine inches wide, those eleven-point-two-five inches long. The house of words was lifted from the floor, carried into new rooms, opened and shut and arranged. It stowed treasure. It flower pressed. It lifted the Zoom Room laptop to acceptable heights. Sometimes just the A through M. Sometimes, also, the N through Z. I slipped spray roses in among the *linnet*, which sing. Pale blue hydrangeas beneath the *drab*, *muddy* of *dunducketty*. Nandina beside the *carob*, that *edible horn-shaped fleshy seed-pod of an evergreen leguminous tree*. I made paper out of books I'd shredded and blendered and lintered and deckled, and I left that paper to dry beneath the reliable weight of the *Shorter Oxford*. Whenever two things had to be fused

(mucilaged)

(adhered)

I knew to trust the house of words.

The battered, resined, cobwebbed, misted *Shorter Oxford* fixing everything.

I will be there, she had said, and I stood waiting, I am waiting.

The *Shorter Oxford* begins with the letter **A**, a and does not leave the letter to itself until it has been exhausted.

Datebook

1992? 1993?	Fae Myenne Ng, Philadelphia Bookstore
Summer (?) 1994	Rosellen Brown and Reginald Gibbons, Spoleto, Italy, Writing Conference
July (?) 1996	Jayne Anne Phillips, William Gass, Gish Jen, and Carolyn Forché, Prague Writing Conference
August (?) 1997	Jayne Anne Phillips and Brooks Hansen, Bread Loaf Writers Conference
1999 (?)	Michael Ondaatje, Free Library of Philadelphia
2006 (?)	Colum McCann, Free Library of Philadelphia
March (?) 2008	Patricia Hampl, Bryn Mawr College
November 15, 2011	Jill Lepore, Lore Kephart '86 Distinguished Lecture Series Speaker, Villanova University
March 19, 2013	Janet Malcolm, Kelly Writers House
March 24, 2015	Dorothy Allison, Kelly Writers House
January 14, 2016	Elizabeth Strout, Free Library of Philadelphia
April 13, 2016	Philip Lopate, Bryn Mawr College
February 22, 2017	Dana Spiotta, Bryn Mawr College
August 25, 2018	Abigail Thomas, Hippocampus Conference, Lancaster, PA

October 8, 2018	Gerald Casey, Penn Book Center
March 7, 2019	Nicole Chung, Blue Stoop and Writers Room, Drexel
March 19, 2019	Carolyn Forché, Free Library of Philadelphia
April 22, 2019	Rosanne Cash, Kelly Writers House
February 22, 2022	Amitov Ghosh, Kelly Writers House
July 13, 2022	Alice Elliott Dark, Free Library of Philadelphia

In time, I got better at keeping a datebook. I left less out. Put more in. Took care with my dark pen.

Understanding

Dear Dard:

About that tortoise.

Already ancient by the time you met it, in the village of Nuku'alofa, on the island of Tongatapu, in the wooden palace of the queen. The year was 1926. You'd traveled miles—from Ohio to San Francisco to Tahiti to the Cook Islands to Wellington, New Zealand, toward the Fiji islands—all accounted for by your complicated crush on what you called "the primitive bark papers of the South Sea Islands."

(*Primitive.* Again, Dard. History will wish you had chosen another word.)

You ached for witness. You wanted to be *in situ* while the women pounded the pale inner bark of the mulberry tree. Smoking as they worked, drinking the pink liquefied flesh of local watermelons, drinking the Kava they had made from the Piper methysticum plant—sieving the sediment with their long hair, then wringing the drink from their hair into the bowls, then sipping, then relaxing into the euphoria. *Have some, Dard.* You wanted to hear the music made in the hands and bodies of the unmachined.

Pounding the bark.

Pounding the bark.

The pounding, and the pounding, and the euphoria, the talk.

In Tongatapu, you in your American clothes and your six-foot posture, you with your effusive curiosity, were first appraised, then welcomed. You were heavied down with gifts—seed beads, you say, mummy apples, cigarettes, mangoes, hand beaters, tapa. You were summoned to meet the queen, and there you were, in those green palace gardens, and there, enclosed by a run of low walls, was the tortoise, Tu'i Malila, a "crusty old palace pet," a Galápagos beast, which had been bestowed upon the island royalty by Captain Cook in 1773, or so the story went. Tu'i Malila had, you write, endured the heat wrath of two forest fires, been cracked by the wheel of a cart, and been disrespected by a horse—kicked in the face by an impatient hoof, so that it had just one eye now, saw only from that side.

You leaned down.

You stroked its head.

And this is what I wonder, Dard: Were you thinking of your own lost eye as you did? The trouble that had begun two years before, when your left eye grew stubbornly unseeing, when, as you write in a letter to a friend, not even $50 worth of treatments could offer any cure, and you were worried that, were your remaining eye to go, you'd have to abandon everything you loved?

Were you thinking about that, your hand on the head of the tortoise?

It must have terrified you, Dard, when your own eye refused to see, when, in November 1924, it hemorrhaged, and hospital surgeons could not save it. You were only forty-one. Your mother would soon die. Your wife, whom you relied on, would take ill. You needed two eyes for deep looking, typesetting, art making, printing—and now you had only one. You'd wanted to give up. You'd considered vanishing into Europe, for as long as it might take to find your joy again, if ever you could find any joy again. You took a long East Coast trip with a friend instead, went home to putter about with new stained-glass windows, recoiled at the possibility of a fleck of flying glass landing in your one good eye, and finally remembered—reclaimed—your obsession with bark papers. That's when you set off for the South Sea Islands in search of the rhythmic pounding.

You write about none of this in your *My Life with Paper*. You keep the fresh terror of the blinded eye to yourself. You don't complain, you don't mourn, you don't make a story of your losing—you leave all of that to Catherine Baker, your someday biographer who will move into your room at Mountain House and read every line of every letter and for three years weigh your tales against the evidence. But there, in the garden with Tu'i Malila, I imagine you imagining yourself to be in the rare company of a creature that might fully apprehend the compounding, tragic halving of a necessary whole vision.

Years later, when you died, on February 20, 1966, of an apparent heart attack, Tu'i Malila was still living. It had met Queen Elizabeth II by then. Its actual age—188 years old? 192?—would soon be disputed, and so would its origin country and its sex. For Tu'i Malila had not, historians say now, been born and bred in the Galapágos. Tu'i Malila was instead a Madagascan radiated tortoise. And maybe Captain Cook himself had not made of it a gift to his island hosts; maybe it was a member of Cook's crew who had left the beast behind. At the very least, Captain Cook did not mention any such tortoise in the written words he leaves behind.

The tortoise itself had nothing to say on the matter. The tortoise kept its secret, grew into its myths, just as you, in writing your autobiography, keep your truest self from the page, so that I did not learn, from you, about your one-eyedness, did not learn, from you, about the ways you loved your Edith, did not learn, from you, about that trick you played within your office in the Charles Hayden Library at MIT, where you adeptly sourced paper fragments brought to you as originating in the war balloons launched by the Japanese. I had to learn how to learn your secrets.

Dear Dard, you were a printer's son; a horseback rider; a chalk talker; a handmaker; a journeyer, an adventurer, a scholar; a son, brother, husband, father, friend; a plaque-earner at the Smithsonian Institution.

But you were also, Dard, an ancient, mislabeled, fabled tortoise's friend, a reptile that only barely outlived you. You understood each other, I believe. You traded silence for silence, myth for myth—your touch upon its head.

What if we could touch the whole of life back and make our pieces fit?

Paper Box

It hid in the living room hutch, third drawer down. Not the Bloomingdale's tie box, not the Bloomingdale's glove box, but the Bloomingdale's shirt box, still with its transparent tissue. The top is checkerboard pearly gray and white, and the word *Bloomingdale's* is lowercased in a bulbous font, just this side of modern. Two brothers launched the "ladies notion" store in 1861. It was subsumed, during the Depression, by Federated. By the time my father left his malodorous job at an oil refinery for a suit-and-tie career and we'd moved to the last house our family would call home, Bloomingdale's had won my mother's heart.

Beneath the tree at Christmas, it was Bloomingdale's, all manner of checkerboard boxes.

In the years following my mother's death, it was still Bloomingdale's—the old boxes emptied of their original purpose and redeployed as provisional cardboard treasure chests. A collection of beads in one. A quick clutch of letters in another. Ribbons. Artifactual miscellany. The gifts themselves had been long dispersed—worn out, faded, tattered. The boxes were the thing.

I was helping my father pack and stage the last house for sale when I found this one. I slipped the lid and folded the thin tissue back. Caught my breath. Stood. Left the amber-lamped living room for the white-bulbed family room where my father sat sifting, sorting, packing—some kind of undercover operation from which I had been strictly banned.

I found this box, I said. *Can I have it?*

Tired, disgruntled, overwhelmed by the marathon that moving had become, my father glared. Breathing asthmatically, he hunched, impatiently shrugged. I took that as permission. I carried the shirt box to the front door and later drove it home.

I had thought that box would tell me stories my mother had not, that it would clatter bridges across our chasms and reinvent the way I loved her. But the stuff in the box that my mother had buried in the third drawer of the hutch, inside squares of wrapping paper and folds of tasseled tablecloths, had not been, I'd come to understand, the original property of my mother. Its contents were not of her curation. The stuff of the box had come, instead, by way of my mother's brother's house, my prized and beloved uncle. For he'd done what we'd all done with our Bloomingdale's Christmases—removed the gift and repurposed the box as a vehicle of safekeeping. Stashed his discontinuous narrative inside a cardboard coffin.

Square, cracked, bent, black-and-white photographs, their corners pinhole-punched. John Bartram High School report cards: my mother's. A notarized deed for the Mount Moriah Cemetery plot. A 1922 certificate of naturalization for Joseph D'Imperio—"51 years old, five feet six inches tall, color: white; complexion: dark; eyes: brown; hair: gray; visible distinguishing marks: none." The *passaporto*, 1870, of Guiseppe D'Imperio of Foggia, Italy, everything written in pencil. An agreement of sale for the house at 6840 Guyer Street in Southwest Philadelphia, made "on the 13th day of June A.D. 1942, with Margaret D'Imperio, wife of Daniel D'Imperio (6841 Guyer St)." My grandmother. My grandfather. My mother and my uncle's parents. Making their big move to an identical rowhouse across their southwest Philadelphia rowhouse street, where my uncle and my mother would—on a small square of open floor—dance the Charleston. Where my grandmother, in the tiny kitchen, would roast her ham, and where, upstairs, in her white bed in her darkened room, she would pass her final days, looking out the front window toward the house they had abandoned.

In his home by the sea, into this Bloomingdale's box, my uncle stashed his story. This was the house that we were strictly not to visit, except for the one time that we did. *Stay close*, my uncle had said on that day, as we timorously and curiously opened the door and stepped into a room of audacious colors and fragile antiques, through the narrow, undecorated kitchen, through to the backyard plot with its single, brand-new tree. *Stay near. Look at only what I show you. Do not climb the steps to go to the secret upstairs inside my secret house.*

My uncle's evidence had been delivered to my mother at some unknown point after his death. The photos, the proofs of bloodlines, the inherited and kept, the corroboration of choices, preference, chance. And now, as well, and of course posthumous, confirmations of and attestations to my uncle's life and death.

The death certificate and its naked facts: "no surviving spouse," "self-employed," "writer," "cardio-respiratory failure," "lethal cardiac arrhythmia."

The obituary: He was an antiques expert, he was an author, he appeared on the *TODAY* show, he was in possession of antique valentines, he had been too busy, he had been quoted saying, for "a special valentine of his own." Alice Faye, he had said, was the last love of his life.

Alice Faye.

The obituary folded so that it would look like trash—yellowed newsprint advertisements on its front-facing back, sloppy creases—

as if whoever had clipped it had read it just once and then rushed it into camouflage, buried the lie, shoved it into the keepsake box: *Alice Faye. The last love of my life.* Crushing the tissue paper. Slamming the checkerboard lid shut. Climbing down the stairs in the split-level house with the single tree in the backyard—the first room vivid, the kitchen so pale—where he had lived, for all those years, beside my uncle, where he had been hiding in the upstairs room on the day we came to visit.

He drove to the post office.

He mailed that box.

It is full of many things and holds few answers.

> *The trade is not a highly skilled one; neither does it, as we shall find, make any special demand upon the strength or nervous energy of the worker. A girl who is neat and quick-fingered can learn the beginning processes more readily, and be advanced to better qualities of work, than a slow-moving girl, or one who is untidy and slovenly.*

This from a 1913 pamphlet titled "Occupations for Philadelphia Girls," prepared by the Consumers' League of Eastern Pennsylvania, which describes, with eerie precision, the labor opportunities for girls considering employment within the paper-box-making industry in Philadelphia.

The writers of the pamphlet purportedly visited all 60 "bonafide" paper-box factories in operation in the city at that time. They describe the work days, typically beginning at 7:30 A.M. and ending at 6:00 P.M., of those "learners, coverers, corner stayers, and hand workers" who would bend and turn scored cardboard or run the covering machines or walk, at day's end, across floors fluttered with scrap paper toward facilities for "tidying up." Weekly wages for girls working in Philadelphia's paper-box factories ranged from $7.51 through $8.86, according to the pamphlet writer, and the best firms offered half holidays on Saturdays.

By the time my mother was buying all those Bloomingdale's boxes, paper-box manufacturing had become a full-scale industrial thing. Still, the box, with its three-dimensions and four neat corners, its reliable tucks and folds, its crispy tissue-papered linings, retains its mystery among secret keepers. A choose-your-ending narrative. A history unfolding.

Ballot

I minded.

How she arrived with signs to be planted in my yard. How she fit the curl of her petitions through the handle of my door. How, with her canvas bag and her comfortable shoes, her causes to defend, her will, she walked the neighborhood with the straight-spine posture of the absolutely sure. How she always seemed to know whom I would be voting for, and how, stepping forward, at the polls, she warned me (it was implicit) toward the better candidates, the ones she, with her surety, chose.

Her eyes were *yes, no, don't you dare*. Her eyes were *I am watching you*.

What did she know about my politically proselytized childhood? My mother in mourning, in memory, in the family room with the TV on, as Richard Milhous Nixon took his final shined-shoes steps across the White House lawn. My mother's untouchable happiness at Ronald Wilson Reagan's inaugural ball. My mother's quiet, forceful joy when the George Herbert Walker Bush letters arrived in the mail, the ones that had been signed right *there*, on the presidential desk alongside the presidential seal.

The president's words in my mother's hands. The presidential *autograph*.

What could the original activist in the comfortable shoes know of the child and then the teen and then the young woman I once was? Of the daughter who grew up wanting not to vote against her mother. Not to cancel her out. Not to dishonor her pleasure. Not to tarnish the exult that had come to her from her chosen presidents.

All those years ago, it was, it seemed to me, indubitable: that to openly align with the original activist would be to launch a betrayal of my mother. Nodding, marching, planting those signs would be choosing neighbor over family. I was a closet liberal self.

Politics is not genetic, but family is culture—a plexus of ideological education, alignments, and expectations; a system, finally, of honor. Love may be a liberation, but it is also an obedience. I wanted to please because I wanted to be loved. I wanted to lock my mother's loving in.

Against signs and slogans, placards and petitions, my heart, when I was younger, hardened. *Do not ask me*, my posture said to the original activist. *Do not force a conversation. Do not expect me to lay my voter registration card down and betray my mother.*

Sometimes now, I surprise myself with the force of my liberal insistence, with the deep intensity of my overt political existence. How I walk to the polling station, briskly, and complete my ballot. How I sit with the news as the day turns to dusk, anxious for truth and angry at liars. How I write my letters and mail them off, buying the local post office out of my favorite rolls of stamps. How I infuse my stories with facsimiles of the world I want. How I sit on the couch in the deep of election night fever-texting my son, fever-texting my friends as the returns come in, certain that my heart will not sustain it.

And how, when I now walk my streets in my comfortable shoes, I look for the original activist. When I see her coming, I stop and wait and then turn in her direction. We have so much to discuss. We have so much to worry about.

In "Rock, Paper, Scissors: How We Used to Vote," a 2008 story in *The New Yorker*, Jill Lepore tells the story of a man named George Kyle, a Baltimore merchant and Democrat, who sets out on Election Day in 1859 "with a bundle of ballots tucked under his arm." This, back then, was the way. It was also dangerous, for those of an opposing party seeking to thwart men like Kyle from voting for the "wrong" party could take any number of steps to interfere. Kyle never did get to the polls that day. He was assaulted by an American Party "ruffian" before he could get there. If the American Party won the count that day, Kyle's assault became just more proof that the election process was in desperate need of actually democratic safeguards. Writes Lepore:

> *Nowhere in the United States in 1859 did election officials provide ballots. Kyle, like everyone else, brought his own. The ballots he carried, preprinted "party tickets," endorsed the slate of Democratic candidates, headed by [William] Harrison. Voters got their ballots either from a partisan, at the polls, or at home, by cutting them out of the newspaper. Then they had to cross through the throngs to climb a platform placed against the wall of a building (voters weren't allowed inside) and pass their ballots through a window and into the hands of an election judge. This was no mean feat, and not only in Baltimore. In the middle decades of the nineteenth century, eighty-nine Americans were killed at the polls during Election Day riots.*

In her book, *This Is What Democracy Looked Like: A Visual History of the Printed Ballot*, Alicia Yin Cheng, galvanized by the ways in which Floridian chads and butterfly ballots dictated the outcome of the *Bush v. Gore* presidential election in December 2020, sets out to collect the often-elusive ephemera surrounding the voice of the people. Along the way, she quotes Philip Loring Allen, who opined, in 1906, that the ballot is "the most potent of all sheets of paper." The ballot is also, of course, one of the most contested sheets of paper, with claims of pandering, money grubbing, and election fraud dating back through the country's very founding.

Luminary

Losing my religion. Not finding myself in that space where I was raised. A Methodist first, and then a Presbyterian, and always a Christian at Christmas.

It's not that I don't believe in God. It's that I have a hard time talking about it all, accepting religion as the profit-loss of tithing, the methodology of institutions, the endless fracture, even the cliques, that frazzle the surface of the fellowship hour.

But I find God in the morning skies that I watch through my bedroom window—never the same light and cloud show, always proof of the ingenious. I find God in the faces of those I love, in the smell of true vanilla, in the giant turtle that once appeared in my yard, as if it had adventured here from distant islands only to waken me to wonder. I find God in the red-tailed hawk that sometimes sits for hours on the high branch of the neighbor's lightning-zipped tree, sentinel of the neighborhood, wildlife for the suburban numb. I find God in the song of rain and in the psalm of an afternoon sleep and in the memories I keep—a brother's oboe, a father's piano, the sound of a mother's sewing Singer.

And I find God in the cold dark of Christmas Eve, in the linear extension of curbside luminaries, street after street, gesturing peace. There will be gifts, but modest ones. There will be meals—my beautiful son, my beautiful husband, my gratitude at our small table. But in the flicker on the streets, in the yield of neighbor toward stranger, in the possibility of a quiet binding, I find my certain peace.

There has been a decree, an imperial demand. Joseph must see where he's going. His espoused wife is on a donkey. A godly child is on the way. The "O Little Town of Bethlehem" is in the distance, and it could be any day now, any minute, and the stars are bright, but still—light their journey. Place the live lanterns at their feet, down the road, down the road, up the road: *this way.*

A story. A tradition transplanted from distant cultures and rising up from the Spanish villages along the Rio Grande. Further adapted. Further spread. *Luminary* is an evolved word. It is Old French, and it is Late Latin. It is "lamp, light-giver, source of light" and "light, torch, lamp, heavenly body."

It is also, according to historians of the tradition, not always the right word for the paper bags we fill with sand so that we might safely plant our candles so that we might safely spark our flames, one bag after the other in the dark. The proper word, in some parts of our world, would be *farolito*, but here, outside Philadelphia, where I live, *luminary* persists. The candles burn toward midnight. The flames lose wick and wax. The light, when no one is watching, snuffs out. Remembering remains.

Blank Book

Watching the birds through the bedroom windows. The zip-velocity of their flight into the berry tree on the eastern edge of the lawn. The eclipsing of their feathers inside the skim of green.

The sun is fur behind fog.

The near air is steam.

—

After my father died and stories left me, I wanted paper, color, thread, ephemera. This I have said. This became the story. I don't mean to poeticize my sudden vacancy. I want only to say that I grew to need the weight of the brayer, the blade, the awl in my hands, the bone folder, and the needle. That I would wake early and climb out of bed and descend into the kitchen, where, on a portable island beneath a warming bulb, I'd squeeze color from tubes onto a crusty Gelli plate and fit what I made into the frame of our one table. I would fold, sew, washi tape. I would slice squares into triangles and edge triangles into squares. Purple sticks of glue. Sticky fingers.

After, I would drink my ginger tea while my husband drank espresso.

—

The birds vanish. They unvanish. The heat is white, and rinsing.

I bought Stonehenge paper, ARCHES paper, bright sulfite, facile newsprint. I bought multiples of the same waxed linen thread because I liked the way hope beat in me when new spools arrived in cellophane. I painted cards. I chain-stitched journals. I sent what I made to my father's friends, and then to friends who had known my father, and then to friends who had not known my father, and then to strangers who did not know me; that is, I filled the mailboxes of neighbors.

It went on like this. Fall, then winter.

I wonder whether birds always know what they want. Whether they know what knowing is.

Alyson answered the lonesomeness I had not known to name. I am not good at gifts, is what she claimed, but her gift—Bhutan Edgeworthia paper of magnificent density—straight broke me. Yellow Tsharsho. Bleached White Tsharsho. Khenpa Tsharsho. Indigo Tsharsho. Tong Fu Tsharsho. Chu Tsharsho. An incomparable luxury.

I designed new shapes of books to honor the gift I had received. New stitchings. New paper. Fuchsia. Navy. Deep green. On the day the box was due to come, I waited at the door, impatiently.

Ruta asked me to explain. I fumbled the vocabulary.

In time, we rearranged the house so that I'd have room to work. Given more space, there was more need. Sharper blades and whole families of awls and stitches growing in complexity. How many scissors do you need? How many rulers? How much paper? How much greed to make the thin, blank things?

The birds plucking their berries from their tree.

In an old barn shelved with split peach crates, I found a book of Russian phrases, and a dictionary of foreign terms, and *Assembly Songs for School and College*. I bought these for my decoratives. At a flea market on a bitter day, I bought Grimm tales illustrated by Maurice Sendak and the Maxfield Parrish iteration of *Arabian Nights*. I turned my duplicate of Virginia Woolf's *Diary Volume One* into material. My auxiliary copies of *Mrs. Jack* and *A Certain Climate*. I bought but could not slice into the airmail letters of last-century war widows.

I collected the leaves of gingko trees, tulip trees, toxic nandina. The cold leather of rhododendron leaves. The soft brush of winterized grasses. I pressed what I'd gathered onto Gelli-plated color, lay down a sheet of ARCHES, and used my fist. Stopped fisting. Peeled.

That was my negative.

I removed the leaves, returned the paper. Fisted harder.

That was my positive.

I never got what I expected.

I wonder whether the berries on the backyard tree would be classified, in the pharmacy of birds, as hallucinogens. I wonder because lately the birds in the rinsing heat have grown excessive in their franticness. They vanish and unvanish with flustering speed. Sometimes, flustering back out into the world, they strike my windowpanes. I rush from the bed to the window and look down, to the ground, to see whether they've survived. They survive, shaking the bruise out of their feathers.

I bought the heavyweight Kozo paper, two hundred grams per square meter (GSM), made from the bark of Thailand trees. The paper they call Chaotic Strings. The papers made with rain tree leaves, with chongco flowers, with bougainvillea, with the bright bursts of pea flowers. The deckle-edged Indian cotton paper. The soft white khadi paper. The Mexican amate bark paper. The Bhutanese Tsharsho paper. The Unryu paper. Four in the morning, unable to sleep, I fell in love, I ordered. And when the paper arrived in its big, long, shallow boxes or its sturdy cylindrical mailers, I felt a kind of joy I hadn't felt for months, and then I felt a kind of greed, and then I bought browning books from centuries ago, piles of old magazines, foreign-language dictionaries, filling my drawers, stacking my tables, with paper.

More waxed linen. More needles—longer, thinner, sensually curved—until Katrina, working by the light of her blue and golden mountain, took fabric culled from distant lives to make me a pincushion. Unheralded, her box arrived. I opened it, astounded.

Then, Bill shaped and baked clay beads, sizing the holes so they would accommodate my needles. He ordered me miniature brass keys and 1928 pharmacy scripts from the Peoples Drug Store in Abingdon, Virginia.

Then, Carolyn sent a box of bookbinding clamps, and a story. After that, she sent a papermaker's frames and screens, tufts of old paper still wedged between them. She sent a bag of crisp dried flowers and instructions on colorfasting.

Then, Ruta remembered a time when she and her brother and sister all lived in L.A. and traveled, on Sunday mornings, to the Rose Bowl flea market. She'd been searching for books, she said, and found buttons instead, hundreds of them, snug in an oblong, nine-inch heavy cardboard Hershey Kisses Chocolate container. A rare delicacy of a box in hues of pink-silver and old-denim blue containing thousands, maybe ten thousand, maybe ten million buttons. Which she sent to me in a box that smelled of smoke, along with two Nancy Drew books, published in 1949 and 1959, and the brown stuff of old tapped-out Western Union paper: *Leaving seven fifty tonight arrive Chicago seven forty five tomorrow night via Northwestern.*

Then, Claire said, *I will show you zinnias.*

Then, Mark said, *Come to my garden. Steal my flowers.*

It's been nearly two years since my father died. The birds vanish, they unvanish, I am watching. They take what they need. They return when they can. The sun leaves the fog. The near steam rises. I make blank books with the paper I'm not hoarding. I send them out from the room where I work, making room for other stories.

At the start of the making of an overhand knot, you hold both ends of the thread in one palm.

In the proper tying of a proper square knot, nothing comes undone.

But the kettle stitch is a mere half hitch, and so it is a danger. It could fail, or you could fail it.

Love is like that.

Also: remembering.

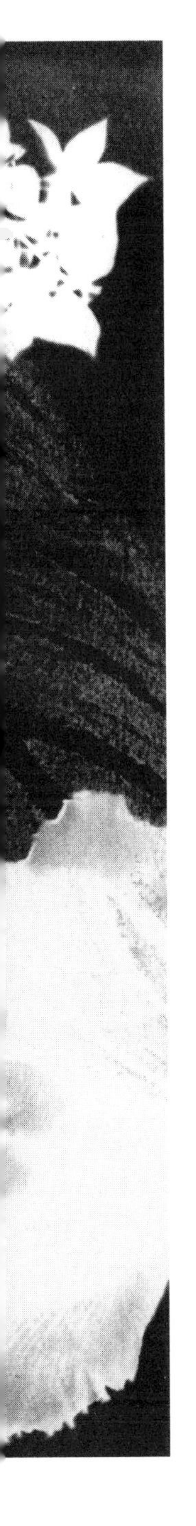

Doubt

Dear Dard:

When you hope and lose. When you lean into the shape of your wish and become its squander. When what might have been is but a dream deferred, a legacy of almost. Will we be remembered for how we yearned or how we finished? For what we effectuated, dispatched, spawned, or for our public forfeitures?

I mean the books I wrote that never sold. I mean the prizes I was not meant for. I mean the ways I wasn't heard, the things I never built, the skills I could not claim as my personal *de rigueur*. I mean your commercial handmade paper mill, Dard, the only one there'd ever be at that particular time in your particular America, except that you could not make it work.

Your *dubious turn*, you called it. Your forty-year odyssey. Your great, absorbing wish. Handmade paper for artisans and books, bearing one of your famous watermarks. It was 1912, and you were twenty-nine years old, when you gave it your first go at Marlborough-on-the-Hudson. Your thatch-roof operation with its waterwheel and screw press, hollander and dipping vat, rag duster and cutter and boiler was too small, and the natural run of water too unreliable, and for two years you worked only to produce paper enough for two books for the Chicago Society of Etchers plus some handcrafted stationery. Your ever-adaptable wife shivered in the Mill House. Your first son was born.

You proposed a second run at it upon your move to Chillicothe, Ohio, but the Hunter Mills never came to pass. In 1928, at the age of forty-five, you tried again. With a business partner's imprimatur, you put $3,000 down for a defunct iron foundry in a ghost of a Connecticut town called Lime Rock. You sent your beaters and molds, vats and tools east by way of a boxcar. You walked the old site, picking through its vast debris, cleaning old bricks so that they might prettily restore a chimney. You oversaw the tedious renovation, ordaining the place with your own stained-glass windows, imagining the beater mash, the aroma of sauced rag fibers, the drying paper hanging like vertical clouds to dry, a little paper museum, right there, by the creek.

(Your sons arriving in the summer months and playing in the splash.)

(Your wife arriving, too; she would be charming.)

You hired skilled men from across the country and the seas—professional vatmen, professional couchers, your version of a salesforce—but everything took much longer than you'd hoped, and your business partner was difficult, the lawsuits got messy, the economy was rarely with you, the eventual receivership was a dose, and too much of the paper the mill did manage to produce was prone to initially invisible diseases, to spots and streaks and grime, to the ghosts of steel-wool hair, as if the paper were possessed. Not all of it, Dard—you had some buyers, some success, enough good output to feed your own book projects—but in too short an order, you had to red flag the operation, proving the theorem you had not set out to prove: that the world's undisputed expert in paper could not finally make paper in the seamless, economically successful manner he had dreamed of.

A brutalizing failure, except that I am holding some of your Lime Rock paper now—the swatch of it that got bound into the book my brother gave me because it was a book my mother wanted. There are many who picked up where you left off, who staked a claim, who decided to make paper. My favorite is the story of Sue Gosin, an artist and papermaker who grew up among commercial papermakers.

It's the mid-1970s when this story begins. Gosin has just received her master of fine arts degree from the University of Wisconsin–Madison, where she had watched New York City artists come and go to learn what they could about the depth and soul of paper, the natural occurrences that became the stuff of the surfaces they worked on. She'd attended a gathering of paper people in Appleton, Wisconsin—had toured your collection then at the Institute of Paper Chemistry, had talked to other enthusiasts in the early throes of the handmade paper renaissance you would have loved to see unfolding.

Imagining what might be, she, with her then-husband, packed her Volkswagen bus, her cats, her dogs and set off for New York City, where she intended to make paper for the artists who needed paper, although first she would have to learn how. She and her husband secured a fifth-floor space in a SoHo loft. They found engineers at the Navy Yard who agreed to design and build them a press. They received a handmade beater from a beloved teacher. The owners of the local garment shops said "Yes" when they went asking for remnant cuttings—the diapers, shirts, dresses, linens they might tear and beat and test. The owners of the shop where they bought fresco pigments became accustomed to their presence. They called their place Dieu Donné, and the artists came, and the nights were wild. Sometimes, they'd put the live lobsters they'd buy at Fulton Market at 4:00 A.M. in their paper vats, leaving the crustaceans alive until they made dinner later.

The thing is, Dard, it worked. At Dieu Donné, they learned to make paper—archival, soulful, vibrant. They learned, too, about the art of collaboration, about what happens if you teach an artist like Chuck Close, say, to think in pulp. Children came to Dieu Donné to be taught the miracle of paper. The country's first university papermaking syllabus emerged. The organization kept growing until it moved to its new home—back to the Navy Yard in Brooklyn, where their first press was made. Maybe it stopped looking possible, from where you stood, all those years ago. But it wasn't, Dard, and without you, it might have never happened. Where does a renaissance begin? Whom should we credit?

If is a word climbing up, falling down. *If* propels, condemns us. It's your grandson, Dard, your second namesake, who keeps your paper safe, in the Chillicothe house where you once lived, who occasionally shows others how to make it. Because sometimes it just takes more time than we have, or more time than we believe we should believe in.

Report Card

If only I could get the A, I would be someone. Just look at the thing, the capital A—how upright it is, how both-arms-rising. The capital A achieves its own pinnacle. It strengthens itself with a bar. It is first among many, the alphabet queen. The A is for smart girls. I want one.

Now that I have the A, I must keep it. Now, my A cannot simply be a veracious stroke of multiple-choice choosing. Or pretty words. Or my civil behavior in the classroom. I have to show flair. I have to get my pronouns straight, be a little original, but never flagrantly outlandish. Who will control the thoughts in my head? Who will sit me in the chair when I'd rather be outside running or inside skating or anywhere but thinking?

Still, I want the A. My brother always gets the A. My brother is the smart one. I trail along, two years behind, scooping up whatever's left of the praise he leaves behind, his easy As, his mostly As plus pluses. The teachers know that I'm not he. They can see straight through me. They detect the falter in my speech. My intelligence (can't fool them) is anything but curvaceous. I am, in fact, of middling mind and anxious soul. My thoughts are currents jumping. I must work for my A. I must perform the extra credit. I must sit in the front row and raise my hand and be never once late with my homework.

Because I do not simply want the A. I want a report card sweep. Something to be proud of. Something that proves my worthiness as the younger sister of the smartest boy in every single class.

At Yale, in the late 1700s, you might be Optimi, second Optimi, Inferiore, or Perjore. At William and Mary, a few years later, you could be "first in [your] respective classes," "orderly, correct and attentive," the sort of student who registered "very little improvement," or one of those unfortunates who had appeared to learn "little or nothing" at all.

Elementary and secondary schools in the United States relied on a hodgepodge of assessment tools up through World War I. Some deployed letters to rank a student's standing. Some took pains to evaluate the "deportment" of each student in their care. "What had emerged by this period was the notion of all classes in a school issuing grades to students, and those grades amounting to an indicator of student ability and achievement," write Jack Schneider and Ethan Hutt in "Making the Grade: A History of the A–F Marking Scheme." "And as that notion became more accepted, grades began to communicate more and more powerfully outside of the school. As they did, however, they would stir up questions among those working *inside* of schools about just how well they were serving their original purpose of aiding learning."

By 1971, the A, B, C, D, and F had become the "traditional" grading scheme, favored by some 80 percent of schools—this despite the fact that a vast majority of teachers did not believe that the grading system spoke most effectively of the students in their classrooms. I know that it never did for me. The As were never natural. The Bs felt more like home. The Cs, rare as they were, became the evidence of shame.

Syllabus

It started, and then it couldn't be stopped, them calling you *Prof,* although every now and then you'd be summoned with *Beth* by the ones who seemed older than the rest, more secure in the democracy of learning, more prone to the sly harassments of insurmountable questions, and more skilled in the electrovalence of teacherly attention. The ones who said, *Be hard on me.* The ones who gibed at the handwriting you left in the margins of their pages and then walked you halfway to the train and practiced being, as you together walked, the people they were becoming.

Shouldn't the strength of your years be the strength of your years? Shouldn't you, yourself, be bedrock?

Everyone, in the end, ends. The curtain, in its rings, on its hooks, is sibilating—drawing across, drawing to, drawing away, you are drawing away, you are losing the window, you are losing your reflection in the window, you have lost the frame.

Advanced Nonfiction Writing: Getting Closer to the Bone of Things
English 135.302
University of Pennsylvania
Spring 2011

We'll be asking questions throughout this section of Creative Nonfiction, and we'll be writing and reading our way toward answers: What do we owe our writing, and what does it owe us? What is the role of imagination in memoir? How is the persona of our nonfiction different from the person we know ourselves to be, and how different should it be? How important is it, really, to distinguish between story and situation? We'll be provoked and inspired by the work of such authors as Patricia Hampl, Lia Purpura, Joan Didion, Julian Barnes, Natalie Goldberg, Grace Paley, William Fiennes, Michael Ondaatje, Vivian Gornick, and Terrence Des Pres. We'll workshop essays, memoirs, and profiles.

Creative Nonfiction
English 135.302
University of Pennsylvania
Spring 2015

"Maybe the best we can do is leave ourselves unprotected . . ." the poet-novelist Forrest Gander has written. "To approach each other and the world with as much vulnerability as we can possibly sustain." In this creative nonfiction workshop, we will be thinking about what it means to tell our personal stories, and how that telling gets done. We'll be reading writers contemplating the act of writing, writers writing their own lives, and writers who reflect on the lives of others. Failure—what it is and how it shapes us—will be a recurrent theme. Students should be prepared to read, to reflect, to take photographs, to find stories inside music, and to write two key papers—a memoir and a narrative profile—as well as a number of small papers and in-class assignments. Our guest writer this semester will be Daniel Menaker, who was the fiction editor for *The New Yorker* for many years and the Executive Editor in Chief of Random House. His most recent book is the memoir, *My Mistake.*

Creative Nonfiction
English 135.302
University of Pennsylvania
Spring 2017

Memory is mysterious; we can't always remember; we often remember wrong; narrative time gets jumbled. And yet many of the best stories ever written erupt from remembered moments, considered "truths," writers who wrangle episodes into place. In this creative nonfiction workshop we will be thinking about what it means to tell our personal stories and how that telling gets done. We'll be reading some of the writers who do this best. Paul Lisicky. Heidi Julavits. Joan Wickersham. Mary-Louise Parker. Sallie Tisdale. Students should be prepared to reflect and discuss, take snapshots, and find stories inside music. Two long projects—a memoir and a long letter—will be required, as will a number of small pieces and in-class assignments. Students will also have the opportunity to meet and talk with the great Paul Lisicky.

Essays, Fragments, Collage: The Art of the Moment
English 135.301
University of Pennsylvania
Spring 2021

Memory arrives in fragments. Truth erupts; it finds us. A button on a sweater flashes us back to a day of gift giving. A childhood book recalls the one who read the tale out loud. In this class we'll explore the moments of our lives through prompts that range from the tactile to the auditory, the documented to the whispered. We'll produce and share miniature essays. We'll create, as a final product, a curated memoir-in-essays. We'll take inspiration from writers such as Margaret Renkl, Charles D'Ambrosio, Durga Chew-Bose,

Elissa Washuta, Brian Doyle, Marc Hamer, and Alexander Chee. The writer Arisa White will join us.

Yearly, with Adjustments

Writers engage with the world around them, and with one another. In this class I will look to you to complete your assignments on time, to participate fully in conversations, to give your all, and to grow. You will be asked to read the assigned material in timely fashion and to complete a series of short pieces—some of them written in the fury of class time and some of them written on your own time. I want you to pay attention to what you are learning and how you are applying what you've learned. I will ask you to look for and defend essays that fall outside the curriculum. After 2022, upon my sudden and heretofore unforeseen retirement, which will be my choice, entirely, which will come as the result of zero administrative pressure, I will no longer be adjusting this message, though I will be perpetually missing the Lovely Ladies, and will be grateful that Brenda Miller was able to join us.

Sometimes there were so many in the teaching room that you ceded your seat at the table and stood for the three hours, softening the patent in the leather of your pink Doc Martens. Sometimes, the distance between the chairs and the walls was no distance at all, so that a student, urgent with pee, would crawl beneath the table, *excuse me, excuse me*, and regain their height on the other side, and make it out the door on time, to the bathroom down the skinny corridor, and we would just keep talking, we were so sure that the student would return to us, we were so sure that the student was ours, belonged to us. Once, we found a mouse in the trap, and once, a formation of fly husks on the sill, like somebody's winged soldiers, and whenever we jiggered the windows open, they would slam shut, spitting their chipped, loose teeth of paint into the room, and this is not a scene, only a situation, and this was that one room only, the room of most of your years, the room that doesn't exist anymore, taking part of your history with it. Because in the first room, in the first year, there were only five of them—loose and jangly and mostly ill at ease—and it was a very different room, and in the last room, the best room, your heart was in smithereens.

Shouldn't each semester exclaim upon the past, rise up, messianic, anticipating the prefatories, forestalling the swerves, proving the sedimentary of intelligence? Shouldn't you say that you are leaving because your mascara ran, because your glasses smogged? You only knew Apple, but the room was IBM PC'd. You could not hear them behind their double COVID masks. Sometimes, when you turned your back, you did not feel their eyes on you.

At the end of those winter days, you could not make your way home from the station. You could not walk another mile in your cracked Doc Marten boots, a hole in the toe of your stockings. The ache in the ankle that will always now be broken. Your age. The weight of your coat on your shoulders, your books in your bag, your unfulfilled intentions, the tonnage of self-doubt. You called for help, and your husband arrived, trailing Jeep rust, that Wrangler with the broken zipper plexiglass windows and the pool of floorboard wet where the snow had blown in. You barely opened the door, and you barely climbed up to the gray fade of the seat, and you barely dropped your bag to the damp floorboard. When you got home, you stumbled up the walk, and through the door, and to the couch. You were catatonic, and your husband, following in your wet footsteps, said, *Look at yourself, remember this.*

—

In the last room, the best room, your heart was wild. This new room was your second chance. They gave it to you, mid-semester. You had begged them. You'd seemed desperate.

—

You said: (a) Contain your passing thoughts. (b) Summon the photograph's negative. (c) Muscle memory. (d) Sonnet your confusion. (e) Jangle your fragments. (f) Delineate your alternative history. (g) Write haunted.

—

You said, right, okay, let's make this easy: Narrative arc. Character arc. Voice. Tone. Mood. Theme. Hierarchies equaling purpose. Writing *to* as a way of writing *of.* The origin impulse as persistently urgent, descriptions as inherently complex, paragraphs operating as poems, structures alive with the impulses of the natural world.

—

You said: A work of writing reflects your mind; don't overthink it. You said: You own the work; the work works for you.

—

A motif might, you said, be birds in flight, in song, in wait. Or the progressive movement of the sun across the room. Or the sound of rain becoming the sound of footsteps becoming the sound of an idea. Or successive bodies of water, or the iterative colors red, or the life of seeds. Or a motif might be the ways in which you repeatedly encounter, and therefore enlarge, the magnitudes of sadness.

Pivot is a word you used: *"Altered Flowers" is the pivot essay in the Brenda Miller collection. In* Who's Your Daddy, *forgiveness is the pivot. Feel your way toward the pivot; the pivot knows that it's the pivot.*

Juxtaposition is a word you sliced: *If hurt sits beside hope, what sits beyond hope? If a black braid becomes a black bird, what happens on the pages in between them? If white space is the pause, what isn't pausing, and in what sequence, and what is the consequence of the sequence?*

They wrote: childhood, yearn, forgiveness, becoming, the cost of pronouns, lipstick, they say|therefore, feet burn, fragments, tripartites of silence, rhyme and no reason, mother of pearls, the relative pleasures of bed, the bruising at the ice rink, the white communion dress, mothers.

They yielded: *Poa arctica*, a purity of wish, escalations of the self, the who they told her to be. Smuckers Uncrustables. Albania. Grandfathers. The silence in the bottom of a pool. A stray droplet of the sea. Arachnophobia. The Bedouin way. An hour north. A body made of stardust. Whipped meringue. The two-step and the glide of truth, and time to each other, for each other, for you, from winter through spring.

You gave them names: The Spectaculars. The Astonishments. The Wows. The Lovely Ladies. You wrote them into your novels, gave them the endings you wanted most for them—the hero's perch, the brain that will not stroke, the heart big enough for the world as they defined it. You asked them what they'd carry forward, and they said: *ideas of community*. They said: *kinship*. They said: *opening the inner monologue to art*. They said: *everyone has their own story*.

Sometimes, you see them now in the world, and they are famous—in the pages of magazines, at the helm of magazines, in the hands of the most important agents, winning prizes. Sometimes, they write to you wanting a letter—a point of access to their third degrees or their fourth careers or their next pretty prizes. Sometimes, they send you something they have written, or the date when they'll be traveling, or an invitation to a cafe table in New Orleans, where no teacher comes between you, only the white, warm dust of beignets.

You don't know how you will feel until you have the time to feel. You must leave to find the time to feel, and then you'll be doing all the feeling, and what if, then, in the molasses mess of your feeling, you will know that the leaving was wrong, that you were not ready, that having time to feel is the condition of remorse, that all you ever really wanted was the time to feel, but not the remorse?

What if, in losing teaching, you lose your Book of Commonplace—the new of the students, the fester in their stories, how their stories became your stories?

—

You'll never name the students you now will never have.

—

It started, and then it couldn't be stopped.

Syllabus (*The New Shorter Oxford*): 1a) A concise statement or table of the headings of a discourse, the subjects of a series of lectures, etc.; a list of contest; an abstract; a summary.

And so many words, to walk away.

Spreadsheet

What. Now? *Suddenly.* They stop.

The deadline days, the to-do ticks, the ideas that had preceded whatever had reliably and rushedly come next—and I think of my father in his hawk-hunch at his desk, his thumb and forefinger cradling his thoughts, his lamplight slashing in from the left, his pens thickened with old ink, and his pencils stubbed, and a nearby coil of FOREVER stamps uncoiling, a perpetuating coil of unsent stamps. My father—twice retired from his final corporate stint (he'd gone back after the first quit; he could not quit) and still, at eighty-six, eighty-seven, eighty-eight, eighty-nine, working phantom jobs.

My father, spreadsheeting the void.

Hey, Dad.

I'm busy.

Just wanted to talk.

Work to do.

I think of my father, who had known himself by the work he'd done, who had reenacted work in retirement days, who had taught the equation, across the expanse of his life, work = worth = you.

Equals me.

And my deadline days are gone.

—

When I open the window, the silence is bird soprano and the fizzle of the red leaves on the branched tree that has grown too strong beside the house. Today, the wind sounds like Jersey Shore wind, on that part of the beach where the gulls swoop and the carcass of a horseshoe crab undulates, alive-like, in a tide pool.

I push the glass up. The wind and its chill enter.

Time.

—

Thesaurus.com lists *lazy*, *loss*, and *failure* as antonyms of *work*—perilous, disreputable words. *Fun* is listed, too, but still: the industrious years being the illustrious years; timesheet hours being utility hours; utility being the purpose. The unfailed. The unlost.

Just an hour, Dad?

Just to talk, Dad?

By his desk in the family house, I'd stand. By his desk in his retirement villa. By his desk in the first room of the two rooms in the independent living quarters, the final stop in his tour of final homes. He'd begun taping his passwords to his computer screen by then. He'd built elaborate filing systems for not forgetting. He'd festooned his couple hundred square feet with ink cartridges and paper clips, mailing labels and FedEx slips, scores of multicolored folders. He'd press the finger and thumb to the thoughts in his head, those thoughts increasingly and only in his head. He'd rotate the spreadsheets, this way and that—empty columns, empty rows.

But, Dad.

—

Today's wind is like the wind on a late-September Jersey day. The cool of it presses against my cheek, and time. I stand in this room. I look about at its drawers and shelves of empty paper—unwritten upon, unstoried paper. Its tins of buttons and clay beads. Its needled pincushion and spools of waxed thread. Its box of messy acrylic paints. Because in the absence of deadlines, tick lists, ideas, I make blank books. In the absence of lists, I stitch.

A concertina book is valleys and peaks; I sew the blankness into each sharp, bone-folded crease. A casebound book hides its binding threads; I brush the glue onto the spine, align, press, wait. A stab-bound book is not nearly as violent as it sounds, although smoke does rise when the drill whees down up down up through the Yellow Tsharsho Edgeworthia, the 6E Hanshi, the Blick sulfite—the afterward air smelling of ash.

I like the harsh and the sweet of the ash.

Now, the sounds in the room are snip pierce pull pause and the songs of the birds in the chill. Now, the sounds in my head are all the ways my father implied, insinuated, never directly said, or was it directly said: work = worth. All the ways he spreadsheet-sighed, his columns and his rows mounting zero.

What is the worth of a blank book?

What might have been the worth of time, of me?

While I was growing up, my father's only genuinely unworked hours were the hours he spent by the sea—warming his chest with the sun, digging his toes through the sand, watching the waves for dolphin fins. Unworking the Jersey Shore. Unworking Hilton Head Island. My father unhunched. I'd sit beside him on the scratch-plastic upholstery of the low beach chair, alerting him to fins. I'd watch him doze as the fore edge of the wave foamed toward and away. I'd keep him safe while the briny air blew, lifting the thin threads of his auburn hair that never finally grayed.

Still, work was the abiding lesson of my becoming—the posture and pose, the language my father spoke most persuasively, the spectacle of his identity. I was a student of his early rise, his briefcase, his late nights, his weekend worries. I postured after him. I posed. I took my first job, retail, when I was sixteen. After that, a mimeograph shop; a catering gig; a library; a Realtor's office; an investment firm; plural architectural interior-design engineering firms; a compensation consultancy; then eighty-hour weeks of freelancing words for the pharmaceutical, real estate, and nonprofit industries; all preliminary to a strange eight-month stint with public broadcast TV. There was writing, then there was teaching, in between.

I was holy unto myself when I was working. I was purposed. I was my father's oldest daughter, and the work that I did was my father's pride in me. My busy was his pride. My late nights. My weekend worries. My early rise. My stumbling, complicated, compiling exhaustions, my inability to confess that what I wanted most was the brine of simply being.

Keep the wish for it unsaid.

Keep the working going.

My father died not far from the fortress of his desk. Not far from his curdled ink and pencil stubs and dented files and quarantined spreadsheets. I held the hand that no longer held his thoughts until he took his final, violent breath. *What are you doing here?* were his last words to me. As if I should be elsewhere, purposed. Elsewhere and unfilled and unlost.

—

In the days afterward, I emptied his two rooms, his drawers, his desk.

I released the hunch of him to the breeze, the thoughts he'd kept in the press of his hand, the voids he'd calculated.

I stole the uncoil of his FOREVER stamps.

I was his first daughter, not a daughter. I was empty columns and empty rows, mounting toward nothing.

—

There is time now. There is the Jersey Shore nature of the breeze. There is all this empty paper in all these empty books, the hidden cheat knots of the coptic stitches, the miniature brass keys I sew into the Khadi paper that sleeves the signatures, the differently complicating exhaustion, the math I cannot do on time, on worth, on me.

Dad, please.

Outside, in the breeze, in the street, a girl has started to scream, abbreviated blasts and bleats that seem designed to test the fierce in her, to articulate her power, to name her place in the scheme of things. A girl who screams only to scream, or that is how it seems to me.

The bookbinding needle goes in, goes through. I pull the waxed linen taut and stop. *What are you doing here? What are you doing?* Pay attention to the sound of the knots, to the birds in their song, to the rustle in the trees. Pay attention to the outside girl. Who stops and now again who screams.

Leave it to a Franciscan to put it all down in a book, to elevate the practice of double-entry bookkeeping inside one chapter of an elegant Guttenberg volume, the title for which does run a tad long: *Summa de Arithmetica Geometria Proportioni et Proportionalita* (1494).

Born in 1445, orphaned and then apprenticed to a Venetian merchant, Luca Pacioli must have been a charmer. Friend to Filippo Brunelleschi and Donatello, patron of the Duke of Urbino's library, tutor to Leonardo da Vinci on the matter of mathematical perspective and proportion, tutor to Albrecht Dürer, scholar, professor, and Francis of Assisi follower, Pacioli had a gift for explaining the perplexing. *Summa* wasn't his only book, but it was highly influential, undergirding, as it did, one of the bedrock tools of capitalism.

Double-entry accounting was the art of credit and debit bookkeeping, a kind of spreadsheeting in which debits and credits never lost sight of one another—each being perpetually balanced against each.

"In the context of the impact of his treatise on double entry bookkeeping, its publication came at a time when the spoken language seldom appeared in print," writes Alan Sangster in "The Life and Works of Luca Pacioli." "The influence of its presentation of that language went far beyond accounting, into the heart of commerce itself."

This balancing, weighing, reconfiguring, reimagining—one entry versus the other—was, I think, my father's favorite thing. So that now, and again tomorrow, and again, I write his history in spreadsheets. I look for myself inside his columns.

Making

Dear Dard:

You trace it back to a poem—here in my country, in my city. You report, in your *Papermaking through Eighteen Centuries*, the first published rhyme written for the colonies by a man named Richard Frame. Frame was annotating Pennsylvania's wonders in his literary survey of 1692, "A Short Description of Pennsilvania, Or, a relation What things are known, enjoyed, and like to be discovered in the said Province." When he arrived, in his expository travels, in Germantown, he dawdled over the spectacular lifecycle of the colonies' first domestic paper:

> The German-Town of which I spoke before,
> Which is, at last, in length one Mile and More,
> Where lives High-German People, and Low-Dutch,
> Whose Trade in weaving Linnin Cloth is much,
> There grows the Flax, as also you may know,
> That from the same they do divide the Tow;
> Their Trade fits well within this Habitation,
> We find Convenience for their Occupation.
> One Trade brings in imployment for another.
> So that we may suppose each Trade a Brother;
> From Linnin Rags good Paper doth derive,
> The first trade keeps the second Trade alive:
> Without the first the second cannot be,
> Therefore since these two can so well agree,
> Convenience doth approve to place them nigh,
> One in the German-Town, 'tother hard by.
> A Paper Mill near German-Town doth stand,
> So that the Flax, which first springs from the Land,

First Flax, then Yarn, and then they must begin,
To weave the same, which they took pains to spin.
Also, when on our backs it is well [worn],
Some of the same remains Ragged and Torn;
Then of those Rags our Paper it is made,
Which in process of time doth waste and fade:
So what comes from the Earth, appeareth plain,
The same in Time returns to Earth again.

America's first paper mill tore and turned and washed on twenty acres along a sliver of water now known as Paper Mill Run. Its creators were William Rittenhouse, a German by birth; William Bradford, a printer in need of paper; and two other investors. Within a decade, the first Rittenhouse structures had been vanquished by a flood—the paper, the machinery, the tools all gone. No matter. The determined Rittenhouse began again, resurrecting the operation on a new spit of land that also proved susceptible to nature's will. Still, the colonies needed their paper for packaging and writing and printing, and the Rittenhouse clan persisted, erecting new structures and machines to facilitate the stamping of the old rags that had been worn by their near neighbors; the washing of the pulped rags with fresh stream water; the forming of the "stuff" by way of molds and deckles; the squeezing of the drippy pages beneath the strong arm of the screw press; the felting, the drying, the sizing, the drying again.

Think of paper hung up in a loft like freshened shirts, waiting for a breeze. Think of the crinkle of it wrapped and twined and sent off in carts to the bookman who was waiting to print, the wife desperate to send a letter, the butcher wanting to package his meat, that Christopher Sauer who was busy producing those German-language bibles that were in such high demand among the Mennonites.

Think, I write to you. As if you need to be encouraged.

How essential it was, how necessary, America's first papermill, and yet, Dard, when you went looking for proof of the operations, the mill had gone up in smoke, like one of Phil's magic tricks. "Nothing remains today of the old handmade paper industry in America as here, though not in the Old World, the advent of the papermaking machine soon swept aside the ancient, tedious method of forming each sheet of paper separately," you write in *Eighteen Centuries*. "Just at the close of the Civil War all paper making by hand had ceased on the North American continent. Most of the buildings that housed the important early industry have gone into decay, and not a vestige of any old equipment, except a few scattered moulds, remains."

It was this, Dard, that you sought to fix, this bygone-ness that you reckoned with. It was this that propelled you toward building those mills of your own—fighting nature and economics and capitalist desire. But even you, Dard, with all your strength and verve and knowledge, could not win against the inevitable. Years after you finally gave up the operation, in 1955, a flood would topple your Lime Rock mill into the Salmon Fell Kill, the pieces remaining like fallen tombstones until, in the name of cleanliness and progress, they were scooped up and carried to the dump.

Before I knew you, Dard, I, too, went searching for the ghosts of the Rittenhouse mill. I received my cursory education on cloth rags, cellulose, lye. I walked the Paper Mill Run. I imagined the seed that grew the flax, the flax that shaped the linens, the old waistcoasts, shifts, petticoats, and aprons being shorn of their hooks and stamped down by machines. Beneath the confetti blossoms of cherry trees and a few white butterflies, six restored structures and an explanatory mill model stood, and somewhere, I was told, was proof of the original structures, discovered during an archeological dig. And then I stood, as school children do, before a reconstituted vat with a mold and deckle in my hands and dug into the "stuff" to form my own sheet of paper. My handmade paper was "rough-edged, an open canvas," I wrote then, for my city's paper. "An invitation to the imagination that will, perhaps someday, absorb my mad dashes, my bad metaphors, my scribbles, my scars, my angsty secrets."

But it wasn't my own imagination, as it turns out, that became my *perhaps someday*. It was you, Dard. Your ghost reeducating my own memory. Your search exacerbating my own. I see the world in new ways now; I understand how we are bound by the mysteries of making.

Wasp Paper

It was hanging on the tree out front, high up, in the old Japanese maple. Hidden in summer by the profusion of leaves. Hidden in fall by autumnal color. Then: rain, wind, winter. One day, I looked up, and there it was—unspectacularly gray and remarkably tenacious, like a boast-less Christmas ornament or light-less Chinese lantern.

I looked out for it as I looked out for the moon, or for the hawk, or for the red, red fox, as if I could protect it. One day, I looked out, and the tree was bare. Whatever had latched the wasp's nest to its skinny branch had snapped. The nest had billowed to the ground. Must have billowed. For when something weighs practically nothing, when something is built of thin partitions between pockets of now-empty cells, how does it fall from a tree? How does it not simply lift up and fly, like a balloon that has escaped its string?

I walked out into the rain. I collected the nest, left it on the porch to dry, and three days later brought it inside to sit in a room that is now decorated by my squares of handmade paper. The nest was of many rooms, a complex symmetry, with a nice rounded roof and a striated facade, and a quality that was remarkably enduring. I could not tell where the queen wasp had gotten her start—where she had laid down her first line of wood-masticated pulp, her body providing the glue. I couldn't tell, either, where the worker wasps had gotten in on the act—after being eggs the queen had made, after maturing, after foraging for supplies and returning to their birthplace as its expansion architects, after the queen had settled in to just sitting there then, laying her eggs and laying her eggs and seeing the nest grow, the thrumming growing nest. No other nest in the world like this one, the watermarking of time and buzz, the ingenuity of instinct.

Nature was the original papermaker. The wasps, yes. Also conferva, which is filamentous green algae, according to a story Dard Hunter shares in *Papermaking through Eighteen Centuries*. I am quoting from Dard's book now, and he is quoting a man named G. A. Senger, who in 1799 published an essay about his gray-green "water wool" on that very "water wool" paper:

> *In my walks on the border of a small brook, I found both shores in the side of the hedges covered with a slimy substance, which the overflowed brook had deposited. The surface of the water was covered anew with a yellowish green vegetation, and in the windings of the stream there lay quantities of this fine vegetable product piled in heaps, which gave additional beauty to the blooming shores of the flowing brook. The appearance of this beauty and the thought of a useful application of this material awakened my interest, for I could not persuade myself that thrifty Nature would have brought forth so much beauty and such a great quantity of the fleecy substance, without its having a useful purpose. This covering extending over the surface of the water, was not only a resting place for insects of various sorts, and a well secured storehouse for their broods, but as Nature intends everywhere to give many advantages, I soon experienced that it contained a proper stuff for the making of paper, and what is more surprising, a paper prepared by Nature alone, without the assistance of imitating processes.*
>
> *This peculiar web contains innumerable fleecy parts of vegetation, which are generated, in the first part of the*

spring, on ponds and other standing waters; they detach themselves from the bottom, and rise on the surface, where they appear as a handsome green and yellow covering. After these fleecy particles have remained for some time on the watery mirror; by the heat of the sun, and by the changing degrees of cold and warmth of the water, they become more united and felted together, bleached, and at last turned into a tough paper-like covering. Or, if this fleecy substance is mixed together, and carried away by sudden inundations, occasioned by heavy rains, and deposited on the shores, it then appears like a thin jelly or slime, which, after it has undergone several changes naturally produced by the contents of air and water, turns into a kind of paper, which resembles the common paper; or, where it has been produced upon clear water, it is not unlike a superior paper, of which some may be adhered nearly as white as writing paper.

Broadsides

It happens on birthdays.

Down into the dark morning of the house I'll sink and then find, resting on my keyboard, an invitation.

Turn me on.

The words referring to the computer.

I flicker it to life. A song starts playing, a video of satin shoes, silk arms, and tango flicks. Ten ballroom lessons for the husband and wife, the video reels, and I play it again and again and again until the husband wakes up.

We're going dancing?

Or a shiny, two-part pot will be nested into a box and I'll lift the lid, unscroll the note, study my husband—the archipelago of his freckles, the white caps of his hair, the hands with which he has made art for all the years I've known him, and for almost all his years before that.

We're learning pottery?

Or here is a macro lens: *Go take pictures*. Or here is a miniature tree: *Plant a garden*. Or here are two red rubber spatulas: *Go bake a cake. Try this.*

Today, we are in the rusted Jeep with the leaking windows and the damp floorboards on our way to Lancaster. Amish signposts. Outlet stores. The sweet haze of summer corn and geometric farmland, silos, the city itself with its central market, its opera house, its proliferation of painted pianos where anyone can sit to perform. This year, the birthday present is three months late, scheduled for tomorrow, 10:00 A.M. Two hours at a letterpress. A typothecarian. Her typothecary.

We eat spiced watermelon for lunch. We explore the edge of the city at night.

The next day, when we knock, she opens her door. We follow her down an unlit hall toward the snap of light. She names the machines she has collected through her typothecary years, tells us their stories: Stoney, the 10×15 Chandler & Price. Mike, the Vandercook #4. James the 10×15 Heidelberg Windmill. Jimmy Jr., which has a lot in common with James. She has been experimenting, in William Morris style, with natural dyes and inks; these are her colors. She has been making broadsides, business cards, greeting cards, art prints; this is her work pinned to the sloop of this string. She stores her type in long, wide drawers or inside open-air shelves, and the drawers and the shelves are oak, and her ears are metal-rimmed.

She instructs us in broadsides. We'll make one each. We'll run the lines of our letters in reverse into the composing stick, lay them out upon a stone, and watch as she, the typothecarian, fills the empty spaces with furniture and then quoins it all tight. Then, we'll mix the inks. We'll roller the ink across the locked-in letters. We'll fit the paper into the grippers of her friendliest machines and pull the levers and watch our ideas curve across the belly of the cylinders. We'll keep a running drawer tab of the letters we've snatched so that we can return them to the right places when we're done.

Bill is always better at the gifts he gives. He tangos persuasively (the women watch). He offers his thrown pots for sale (the people buy). He's better at this, too—hunting through the clinking type, measuring picas, sifting serifs, asking questions: What do you think of *this*? Where can I find *that*? What would happen *if*? I listen to him ask. I listen to her answer. They are going on without me, and I'm just standing where I'm standing, wanting, more than ever, words.

If Not Now,

When?

Bill broadsides.

the

weight

OF HER

WORDS

I ink.

Broadsides, according to the famed bibliophile A. S. W. Rosenbach, were the "first stop-press bulletins. . . . The entire history of America can be written from them, because they may be studied from the year 1639, when the first printing shop was established in this country." Broadsides could be printed with relative ease. They could be distributed, hand to hand, pronounced, denounced, debated. They were proof of discontent, a movement, a regulation, an indoctrination, the birth of a new country. They were what was at stake, what people stood for.

"I would put aside the most exciting detective story ever written to read any Revolutionary sheet," writes Rosenbach in "Extra! Extra!," a chapter in his *A Book Hunter's Holiday: Adventures with Books and Manuscripts*, "for though mere scraps of paper they are filled with magic which interprets the era in sharp, broad lines that the years can never soften. Yes, they are the real pulse of the day and throb with the news of the moment."

Still, we declare. We hope our words will matter. We make what we make, and won't someone please hear us?

Pulp

I tore the story of my life, my book, my memoir in pieces, all to pieces. The signatures from their glue, the sentences from their paragraphs, the metaphors from their performatives, the parts of the letters from the parts of the letters until the book I had written was nothing but confetti, a heap of half words and lost phrases.

There were more copies to tear. I tore them.

Using my fingers. Using my thumbs. No tear quite like the last tear. Every rough edge its own riven rough edge. The heap of my life now a hill of soft rubble, now a mountain, now a massif. Wider. Taller. Faster. More.

The sound of the tearing. The onomatopoeia. *Rip.* Watching my own thoughts fall from my hands like a fast-escaping dream. *It was who? It was when? Why were you running? From grief? To?* I tore until I was done tearing. I hauled my hard labor into the kitchen. I nursed my fingertips, the parts of my thumbs that ached from the tearing. I jammed fistfuls of the errata into a $20 blender, added two-and-a-quarter cups of water, sprinkled in husks of dried tree-peony buds, then played the keys of the cheap machine like a miniature piano. Starting with Milkshake. Moving to Fruit Smoothie. Up to Frozen Drink and back down the scales again to Milkshake, upping the Milkshake to High, to intensify the whirl.

Two minutes like this, three, all that tremble on the kitchen counter. It might have been oatmeal with a dash of red berry inside that blender, it might have been a poultice, but it was paper pulp with accents of tree peony. It was letters, it was shreds, it was the thoughts on the life I had once had—imploded, coagulating.

I poured the stuff of it into a fresh bed of water, over a papermaking screen. I raised the screen, admired the deckle, listened to the excess water fall. I lay the screen with its pulp and its deckle and torn peony inside a baking pan and used my palms and a sponge and two crusty couch sheets and next a slab of wood to siphon off more of the most persistent water.

More ache in my hands, in my fingers.

More water, still, in the pulp.

I carried what I had made through the kitchen, through the laundry room, to the deck, to the sun. I left it to dry beneath the overarch fringe of a Japanese maple, which dropped its seeds, strategic.

Bugs walked across my life. The sun came down upon it, slant. A breeze breathed. I buckled.

Lint, nettles, and hops. Asbestos. The pappas of poplar trees, the bark of mulberry trees, reed grass, and dandelion roots. Potatoes, aloe, sawdust. Lime-tree bark and moss. Seaweed. Turnips. Radishes. Thistles. St. John's wort. Cabbage stalks.

Just ask Dard, who tried to read (and also collect) every book there ever was on the craft of making paper—up to a certain publication year, at any rate, when even Dard could not keep up. He admired the old handmakers who chose to write the ways of their craft down. He scrutinized their words, their innovations, their bound pages. He felt at home with such men as Dr. Jacob Christian

Schäffer, an eighteenth-century German botanist, mycologist, theologist, and ornithologist (among other *-gists*) who had an idea about paper while one day taking a walk. *Bark?* he wondered? *Hemp? Straw? Tulips? Linden wood? Indian corn husks? Did paper,* Schäffer pondered further, *have to be made of old clothes, of which there were never enough?* Why not ask nature in its more raw form to relieve some pressure on the growing paper supply-and-demand gap?

I imagine Dard reading Schäffer's story. I imagine Dard electrified. This is history, and history is personal, and history, from Dard's type, spills. History, in Dard's hands, cannot be contained, it continues:

> *When it got to be expensive asking a local paper maker to run experiments for him, Schäffer sought instruction in the craft, bought himself some moulds, and built himself a minor stamping mill, which he operated by hand. He got to work making paper that was sometimes knotty and dark, and sometimes smooth and nearly white, and sometimes greenish or perhaps lacy. Paper that worked as paper, or did not. Paper that still relied, but to just a small degree, on admixtures of rag fiber.*

Schäffer, Dard tells us, shared what he discovered there at the stamping mill in a series of small-run publications, into which he bound his own paper samples. It was because of his work that an entirely new era of papermaking experiments got underway. One such papermaking pioneer was Pierre Alexandre Léorier Delisle (1744–1826), a Frenchman in charge of a paper mill in a place called Langlée. Delisle would ultimately succeed in the making of what is now called "all-vegetal" paper, using marshmallow, couch root, sponge, willow bark, and absolutely no rag filler—binding the product of his experiments into the backs of books. One copy of one such book found its way, of course, to Dard, its pages, in Dard's words, "a little discolored" but "crisp and well-preserved."

Which is precisely how I would describe the pages of the book that sits beside me as I write these words—Dard's own *Papermaking through Eighteen Centuries*, featuring this Schäffer and this Delisle and a vast cast of other papermaking heroes. I own the first edition of this Dard book, published in 1930 by William Edwin Rudge on paper from Dard's own mill. I wonder, as I turn each page, what Dard would think of becoming his own rare edition, what Dard would think if he knew that I was here, imagining him reading others' stories.

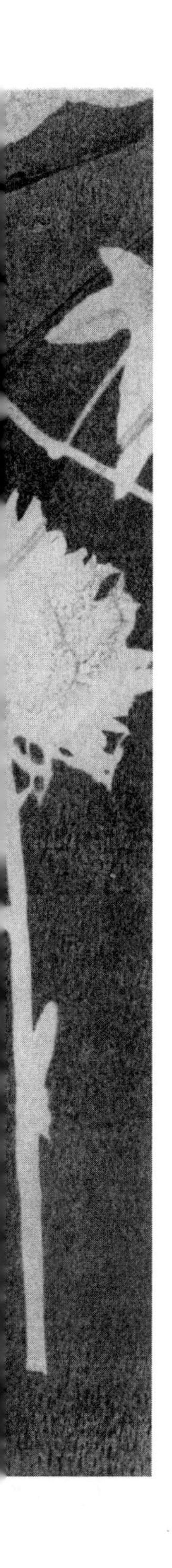

Love

Dear Dard:

Her assertion is in her hands, in her Rachmaninoff fingers. Her history is there, her capacity for applause, though you, Dard, never once, in all your pages, allow us to *hear*, invite us to *feel*, her accelerando, energico, rubato. You do not put us in their audience. You do not record their phrasing, their curl and slash, their summertime trill and winter solace, their evocation, mood, or tremble.

Doesn't take a scholar to see: You barely activate your verbs on the rare occasions when your wife slips into your autobiography. You, who boisterously annotates the village of Kalpi, lavishly captions the deloewang paper of Madoera, romanticizes mulberry, eroticizes the foreign women leaning down and serving tea, and declares your mother to be the one person who actually understands your "exertions," give us nothing but the perfunctory on Helen Edith Cornell. She is an accomplished pianist performing at Roycroft when you meet. Next, she is Mrs. Hunter. Now, you have embarked on travels—Italy, Morocco, Algeria, Egypt, Austria—and now, she is taking piano lessons while you try to talk your way into a Viennese education. Now, she is enduring the frigid cold of Marlborough, New York (enduring it while pregnant), and now, she is hoping you will not continue with your experiment of making "spurious" banknotes. Now, she has moved with you to Chillicothe, and now, there is not one child but two, and now, she is gone. There's so little of your Edith in your *My Life with Paper* that she does not warrant a line of type in the otherwise comprehensive index that would become your final flourish.

We find hints of Edith in other people's stories and in the private hyperbole of your letters and in the hard work of your official biographer, Catherine Baker. We study a pencil sketch, a photograph, in search of aura. We hold fast to the anecdotes we rustle up through our seriously invasive searching: She grew a yellow canary "from seed." She was addicted to bridge. She encouraged her first son to become a philatelist. She was a Christian Scientist whose prayers for Dard II did not save him from the rupture of his appendix; modern medicine, most miraculously, did. She took on your correspondence when you could not see, thought that you should allow yourself to become the subject of a Sterling Lord biography (you said no). She was present when you lost your mother. She tipped paper samples and facsimiles into a book of yours. She (I like this part, I want to meet this Edith) got a job in a capacitors factory to do her part on behalf of World War II—to the factory she went, to the opera, then back home, all while you did your thing at the paper museum of MIT. She loved to drive and you did not, she cooked and you refused, and as soon as you were home from one of your epic trips away, she was off on her own adventure.

See you?

There's chicken in the icebox?

Don't forget to clean?

Tell Cornell to do his homework?

What did she say, Dard? How did she say it? What posture did she bring to her conversations, what smelled like her, what *was* her, what was the color of your soul when she filled your home with song, and when you were lonesome, as you sometimes would admit to being in the midst of a long journey, what did that word *lonesome* mean? What were you lonesome *for*? Are your radical omissions an oversight or your most sacramental act of love?

I am leaning to the right of that equation. I am centering my concluding around this story that your son once told: Your hand-cut type enraged you. It was uneven and inconsistent, and you could not get it to sit just right, and one day, filled with the fury of imperfection, desperately wishing that you were every man and every woman and every talent and every skill in a William Morris workshop, you reached for your hammer. It was Edith, according to the story told, who covered "the type in the bed of the press" with her hands, her Rachmaninoff hands, so that you would not destroy it.

No, Dard.

Stop.

Because she must have known, Dard, that you wouldn't have hurt her. She must have known that she could save you from yourself, that she had that power over you, that your feelings for her would stave off the worst of your poor, conflated instincts. I'm calling that love, Dard. I'm calling that true. I'm calling the stories we don't write our most discretely sacred and the stories we do write the ones that live beyond us.

Postcard

Because he did not have a phone. Because his car was tin. Because neither English nor Spanish was his first language; art was. Because the letters I wrote to him were slanted, dense, salted, a little fisty, and who had time to parse them, reiterate, reflect, react, return, reassure—*reassure* is the word. Because he had torn his 140-pound, natural-finish ARCHES paper into 7.5 × 5.5 rectangles, and because he had a jar of water on his midnight desk, and because he had a thin-haired brush and a few tins of Winsor & Newton paints, and because what he painted was his language, don't say *love.* Say pink skies, ghost trees, terra cotta, the slip of a moon now slipping, pale pink hearts dunked into the crest of a storming sea. Or cloudscape.

How he knew to remember me.

How I knew he remembered.

It's radical, on the face of it—sending your love through the mail, open-faced and defenseless. A postcard is an invitation to any prying eyes. Into a slot, the words and pictures go, into a carrier's hands, through the rumble of sort-and-straighten-and-cancellation machines, into the carrier's truck or bag, until, worse for its wear, it arrives. Its news is old news, except to the recipient.

The first commercially produced postal card—a plain card with room for a stamp and address on one side and printed matter on the other—was, history reports, the brain child of a Philadelphian named John P. Charlton. Others had slipped unsealed notes through the mail before, but Charlton wanted to turn the postal card into a booming enterprise, and so, in 1861, he sold the rights to his idea to envelope magnate Hymen Lipman, for whom Charlton had once worked. The true test of the Lipman Cards would have to wait until the cessation of the Civil War. According to Bob Toal, writing in *Postcard History*, Lipman began advertising a version of his card in the *Philadelphia Inquirer* in the spring of 1872, with the hope of inducing business owners to see the value of the cheaper, quicker, "lighter," medium for getting their news and offers out.

It wasn't long before the postcard transcended utility and became a kind of art, as entrepreneurs around the world applied new printing techniques and possibilities to image-rich heavy-stocked cards that captured a time and place, an idea or sentiment. By the turn of the twentieth century, postcards had become entrenched, indoctrinating correspondents in the art of brevity long before the character mandates of the tweet.

Certificate

In the chapel: My father and my mother, my best friend, my brother, and my sister, the flower lady.

Not in the chapel: The groom and his brother.

The minister said that my father should, for the purposes of rehearsing, stand in for the man I planned to marry. My father nodded, took my hands in his, and said, so no one else could hear, *You don't have to marry him. There's still time to cancel.*

It rained the next day. The groom appeared.

I have the paper to prove it.

—

But he's so beautiful. But when he's near, I can't stop staring. His chin is not my chin, his eyes are not my eyes, his nose is not my nose, he laughs like no one I have ever heard, he lives according to a motto—*There are no failures in life, just different levels of success.* Few who see us together would guess that I'm his mom.

But I have the paper to prove it.

Certificate (*The New Shorter Oxford*): 1) The action or fact of certifying or giving assurance; certification, attestation. 2) A document in which a fact is formally certified or attested; esp. one formally attesting status, medical condition, abilities, fulfillment of requirements, ownership of shares, etc.; a license.

But why did I need the assurance?

Gift Wrap

I just pretended otherwise. Didn't let myself let on. She couldn't be dying, so she wouldn't be dying, so I bought her Christmas presents. A lidded tureen the color of pale pea soup (Crate & Barrel). A set of baking dishes (Williams Sonoma). A glass and glitter harp-shaped ornament (Waterloo Gardens). Elvis Presley snow-time music ("I'll Be Home for Christmas"). A sweater someone would have had to dress her in, while she lay in her hospital coma, wasn't it a coma, what else would it have been, what is the next word for a stroke, a word that sounds fast and moves slow, so terrifyingly slow, you are watching it happen, and you can't stop it.

I wrapped those presents. I stored them under my tree. I drove to see her beneath the sterilizing lights in that horseshoe of acute care, stood beside her, held her hand, said, *Wait until you see what I got you.*

Wait until you see.

The haze of it, vast and white and gray as a winter sea. The circumstance calling for a massive intervention because Christmas was her favorite season, and I'd bought gifts for her to keep. I'd wrapped in the language of my love. Repair. Redeem. A pale tureen. Her name on the gift tags: Mom.

They sold greeting cards and three colors of tissue paper. It was the height of the Christmas season. And one winter day in 1917, when the Kansas City stationery shop ran out of the tissue, Rollie Hall set off to the manufacturing plant in search of a substitute.

He returned with a stack of envelope liners—brilliantly hued, pleasantly patterned—and priced them at ten cents a sheet. The year was 1917. The now-booming industry of gift wrap had been born. Within two years, Rollie and his brother were designing and producing their own gift wrap. Then came Hallmark ribbons. Then came the invention of the traveling "gift-wrap stylist"—multiple women who all shared the sobriquet Kaye King—who went from town to town, showing off the art of beautifying presents. Creasing perfect corners, behatting boxes, praising the instructional power of the Hallmark booklet "Gifts Too Pretty to Open," and judging gift-wrap contests, the Kaye Kings became minor celebrities, dazzling such reporters as Ruth Wagner of the *Washington Post and Times Herald*, who wrote on June 12, 1960:

> *Miss King is a fresh-faced young blonde with considerable artistic talent. She started out as a simple artist with Hallmark several years ago but got interested in the three-dimensional art of wrapping and now spends her time creating fascinating package ideas using huge pompon bows, roses, lilies, Christmas trees, wedding bells, Easter bunnies and butterflies, all made of paper ribbon.*

Wait until you see, I said to my mother. *Don't leave* is what I meant. As if my pretty packages could save her. As if I could finally fix us.

Prescription

God damn them, Dad. Giving you all the pills you did not need, and extra doses of them. Heart pills, but your heart was fine. Sleeping pills, but your thoughts kept scraping. So many steroids that you could have flown sky high in your own fire-blasted hot-air balloon, but actually, Dad, you were crashing. You were hallucinating, aggravating, hurting.

What the hell, I said, to that doctor. He turned his back on me, he wouldn't listen. *What are you doing to my father?* I demanded answers. I wanted to know why he had poisoned you with outrage quantities of mis-prescribed prescriptions. I lifted my fist. I pointed to the prescriptions. It was a flu, Dad, and you were having trouble breathing. You needed precise help, not every pill that doctor had a name for.

He hurt your head, Dad. He hurt it *permanently*.

I counted the days with you. I monitored the tapering of the doses until, at last, you were steroid liberated, until, at least, we could hope that your body would regain its balance, that your thoughts would stop whirling, that you would sleep again, regain survivable levels of blood pressure and blood sugar. I was there with you, I was helping you think through it, I was in and out and in and out and, on just the day at just the hour when your nurse arrived with your new week of pill packets, I was there, Dad. Beside you.

I studied the notations. I read the words that meant "more steroids." I ran after the nurse before he was out of your room and demanded an explanation: *Why more steroids?*

The nurse sighed; he took a second look. He was nonchalant. He shrugged. *Oh*, he said. *Those aren't your father's pills. Those are the pills of another patient.*

The rage I felt, Dad.

The impotency.

The fact that only strange luck saved you from another round of awful.

Later, a woman would become your doctor. She would oversee the pill dispensers. She would become my friend. Later, Dad, you would be blessed by a woman named Clare, who cared for you as no one could, as I wasn't allowed to, thanks to COVID.

You were loved, Dad. We tried to save you.

Sometimes, I will find a package from Bill—ephemera from another era. The transparent sheafs of an old Japanese newspaper. War-time letters. The pages from a broken book. And, once, an envelope of late 1920–era prescriptions. Cryptic, fading, some of the edges burned, every prescription is its own hieroglyph. Stories no one can tell me.

What the doctors got right. What went devastatingly wrong. Whatever happened to the patients.

At the turn of the twentieth century, Julia Pearl Hughes, a pharmacist educated at Howard University and the Philadelphia College of Pharmacy, wrote, in a letter, of the barriers she hurdled to enter the pharmacy world. Shortly after this letter was penned, she became the first black woman to open her own pharmacy, Hughes Pharmacy, located at 937 Christian Street in South Philadelphia. She would move on in time, becoming a vocal advocate for rights, launching a hair-care line, starting and managing a newspaper. But in her youth, Hughes worked harder than most others had to for the right to receive, translate, and fill the scripts that doctors dashed off for patients.

Her words:

> *My first desire to study pharmacy arose not so much from my knowledge, then, of the very enhancing inducements the profession offered, but with some of the new woman's characteristics and ambitions. I have had from my earliest remembrance the greatest desire to enter some of the professions which seemed entirely filled by the men when there is no reason save a selfish one—why the woman should be excluded.*
>
> *Being a native of North Carolina, I found the professional advantages for women indeed limited. After considering my physical and intellectual ability together with my secret admiration for a business life, I decided to study pharmacy.*
>
> *I first applied for entrance in Leonard Medical School, at Raleigh, N.C. I was refused admittance because of my sex. This only stimulated my desires and efforts for the profession. During the next year I read many of the pharmaceutical works and received some practical help. In the fall of 1895 I entered the pharmaceutical department of Howard University, at Washington, D.C. There I realized I labored under two disadvantages, at least. First, being a negro debarred me from obtaining work in some of the white drug stores, which are greatly in the majority; second, being a female, proprietors seemed to doubt even my ability to learn the trade, and as they had never employed a female druggist*

or an apprentice, of course, I was not made an exception to their rules.

My efforts did not stop here, and through the kindness of the surgeon in chief and the pharmacist of Freedman's Hospital, I was given daily practice in the Hospital Drug Store in which I worked during my two years' course. After my graduation in May, 1897, I accepted at once the position offered me as druggist in the pharmacy of the Frederick Douglass Memorial Hospital and Training School, at Philadelphia, where I still have charge.

My interest and ambition for more knowledge and advancement grows with my work and with time.

I heartily endorse the idea of our young women becoming pharmacists and feel that our fewness in number does not arise from our inability but from a lack of opportunity and encouragement.

Why would any of us want anything less than professionals who are urgent with their caring?

Confidence

Dear Dard:

Did you have a devotee at the *New York Times*? A paper-enthusiast stalker? Or did you write the words yourself—slip a friend a press release and then watch your words appear as news?

There's the all-caps-italics-bold headline: ***EXPERT READY TO SAIL ON NEW PAPER SEARCH.***

There's the little less shout in the deck: *Dard Hunter Leaving Tomorrow for India to Get Data and Actual Pages of New Book.*

There's the lede, in which Dard Hunter is named the "paper expert of Chillicothe, Ohio."

There's the nut graf, in which the promise of a Gandhi visit is sensationally teased with the sort of language I imagine that only you might write.

And there's so much self-promotion about the forthcoming Pynson Printers book that the overwhelming message is clear: Order now. Those who shilly-shally will be sorry.

Off you go, across the seas. You are fifty-four, the age, you say, that your father was when he passed away, and if you are famously modest about your own self, you never mind giving your paper books a boost. There are half a dozen missionaries—and no other paying passengers—on your ship, and once you disembark, five roiling weeks later, you will endure, in casual order, a thirty-four-hour train trip across the Indian desert, dusty footpaths, muddy footpaths, nearly impassable footpaths, and an evening you describe as only you can—your words accelerating horror and humor—in a most unusual lodging. From your own *My Life with Paper*:

> Perhaps the most unsavory feature of the combo dining- and living-room was the system of sewage disposal. This consisted of an open U-shaped miniature canal that ran across the tile floor past the dining-tables and lounging chairs. Although the top edges of this shallow trough were level with the floor one had to be on alert, for it formed a stumbling-place for the unwary. While having a meal it was disconcerting to hear the flushing action of one of the toilets and to be aware that within a few moments a somewhat unpleasant sight would flow alongside the dining-table through the open tile channel, en route to the downspout on the outside of the building. It seemed to me at the time that whoever planned this hotel had overlooked a few minor details that could have been arranged more tastefully.

Nonetheless. You carry on. You tour the Taj Mahal, impatient. You see the local treasures, but that's not the point. The point is, and will always be, paper and the people who make it, and on this trip this (in part) means the macerating, molding, drying, and finishing that is part of Gandhi's dream to make of India a country equipped to produce paper on its own, a country adequately employing its poor to useful means.

You sleep in a train station. You drink buffalo milk. You drag your nineteen pieces of luggage on and on, your trusty guide, Mr. Rao, at your side. Finally, you make it to Wardha, where Gandhi has recently returned to his home among the workshops of the Indian National Congress.

Gandhi will not see you, you are told.

You didn't travel all this way to see Gandhi, you say. You traveled all this way to see Gandhi's *papermaking school.*

Again, you are cautioned: You will not see Gandhi.

Again, you explain: You came for paper.

No harumph. No arrogance.

And now, following your tour of the papermaking school, you are summoned. Gandhi, the man who would not see you, wants to see you. Gandhi—frail, unwell, and indisposed—seeks the company of the great paper-hunting expert who endured the unpleasant, who will ultimately travel India by boat, by car, by train, by foot, by moment, so as to write a book that will sell out after just three hundred copies.

Alongside specialty dates and eggs and peaches, you take your place in the back of a Model T, and the engine turns, and you watch the six miles of passing road until the T stops alongside a thatch-roof house. Wait for the signal, you are told, and so you wait—touring the nearby workshop, taking notes, rendering the eggs that had sat beside you in the T sterile, for that is the only way Gandhi will eat his eggs, because those eggs and those dates and those peaches were for Gandhi all along—backseat largesse.

Here, a man says, handing you a darning needle.

And you poke through the shells of the eggs, making the most of your careful craft hands.

Until, Dard, the signal comes, and you walk, accompanied, to Gandhi's modest home, and you step, stooping, across the threshold, and you are there, with Gandhi, his body as thin as the sheet he is wrapped in, his head upon a pillow, his most trusted disciples on the floor at his side, writing his every word down on their paper. When he sees you, he remarks on your height, on the fact of your stooping. When he extends his hand toward you, you kneel. When you talk, you talk only about papermaking and papermaking tools, about the things hands can do, about that which binds you, man to man, Indian to American, the universal stuff of paper.

When it is time to leave, for Gandhi is fading fast, you take his hand again. You back out of the room in a crouch, so that you don't knock your head in the process. You inhale and you exhale what has just happened here, concluding, with an expert's precision, that you have "indeed come into contact with a 'Great Soul'—the meaning of Mahatma."

Then, you will write the story down and send it away, in a luscious letter to your mysterious Edith. Then, years later, you will write the story again into your autobiography, but you will not materially stray, Dard, from the lines of your original letter. You will not amplify, you will hardly delete, you will barely rearrange the story as you first told it. You will not make room for new news from the past, for any shift in perspective.

As if we can only ever trust the first telling of our tales, when the hand that writes is the hand that still feels the weight of the story within it. As if we can ever see ourselves, Dard, as the world will choose to see us.

Diploma

VNIVERSITAS

PENNSYLVANIENSIS

OMNIBVS HAS LITTERAS LECTVRIS SALVTEM DICIT

Cum academiis antiquus mos sit scientiis litterisve
humanioribus excultos titulo iusto condecorare
nos igitur auctoritate Curatorum nobis commissa

BETH ELLEN KEPHART

ob studia a Professoribus approbata ad gradum

BACCALAVREAE ARTIVM

. . .

Hic Gradvs Praeclarvs In Historia Et Sociologia Scientiae
Conlatvs Est Magna Cvm Lavde

You're pretty sure you don't deserve it. That if you applied today to that very institution, you would be rejected. You should never have been there, either way, for you were a naïf on an urban campus. Let it be known that when your roommate's friend perched in the open window on the fourth-floor ledge of your room in the Quad and, LSD-minded, threatened to fly straight down to Spruce Street, you did not have a plan, only shouted, *No! Don't do it!* That when a roommate was convulsing in the immediate hour, your grand idea was to call her parents, many miles and a few states away. That when a boy you'd met at a party scaled the walls of that same stony building and climbed in through your open window and threw himself upon you in the blanket of the night, you held the trauma close and did not know how and why to speak it. That in the aftermath of all of this, you took to the streets and started walking into neighborhoods where you were not wanted.

You were a university girl, flaunting her tatter.

You see what I mean? You weren't ready. You didn't have the requisite skills to dismiss the boy who sat outside your room and followed you, his shag hair hanging, across the brick-and-ivy campus. You didn't have the language when another boy climbed to the top of his fraternity house and threatened to jump unless you'd date him. You didn't stop yourself from starving yourself, and you didn't stand up to the professor who ridiculed your exegesis of the Wordsworth poem "Nutting." You just never took another English class, which is to say that that was you, basking in the humiliation.

What did you do with your education? Why must you work through your catalog of embarrassments before you see yourself in the vast auditorium perked up with love for Dr. Riasanovsky and his Russian history? Before you remember the you who plunked herself down at the oval in Dr. Kohler's class and half-raised your hand because you had answers to his questions. Or the you in the sanctuary quiet of the Van Pelt stacks, your inky notecards spread before you, your thesis expanding and expounding.

You fought yourself back to a B in biology, after you were sure that you would fail. You wrote every set of lecture notes twice, into separate notebooks, to improve your understanding. You tore your onionskin from your Selectric typewriter when you could write a better sentence. The shag-haired boy gave up on you, and so you started breathing.

Slip your diploma from the shelf where it lies stealthily between the books you never read. Buff the face of the glass that preserves it with a cloth. Bring the pretty Latin close. Be gracious. Take possession. Your Baccalavreae Artivm is because you did not quit. Your magna cum laude is because you learned to appease a fretful mind with knowledge.

Diploma: From the Greek *diploma*: A letter folded double.

Draft

If she writes the story the way she wants to write the story—the guttural cry, the injustice exclamation mark—someone will get hurt. Broken, even. Things break.

If she lays out the plot lines in the order of their occurrence—the momentum building, the inevitability rising, the just before and all the moments after—what will she have? The truth, and also the lie. There are multiple plot lines. They tangle.

Better to tell the story as allegory or camouflage, where *x* never precisely equals *y*, and the facts collide until there are no facts, and innuendo might be accusation (but if it is, the camo will contain the secret), all of which, come to think of it, is the stuff of autofiction. Although she'd like to write that the paint was blue and not red, because red is a completely different story, and not to use the proper pronouns will confuse the pronouns, and weather is ultimately both temperature and mood, so she'll have to keep the weather.

Better, then, to go with comedy—to turn the whole blare of the incident on its waggish head. There's the chance (give her a few days) that she could find some humor in it. That she could render the day itself a circus and then lean on circus metaphors—the big rent-a-tent where the scene went down, the daring trapeze (flyer, catcher), the clown that she imagines she was in the moment between the before and the after, with her tripping slap-slap of shoes, and her arms flapped out (flap-flap) for the balance that does not come; she is still, now, on the short stone wall flapping her arms, searching for balance, and the bone has not yet cracked, she has not yet heard it cracking—but maybe the circus metaphor is overdone, and besides, comedy is a truther's stretch—inaccurate, bungling, and boggling.

Probably best, then, to go with grace. To write of how, now, she lies on the couch at night while her husband lies in the room above her, a boot the size of an elephant leg encasing the bone that broke and slowly is healing. She lies there, alone, and the night breezes in, the end-of-summer cicadas, the hoof beats of the deer near the hosta they have, stem by stem, been stealing. She lies there listening to the dark, and the ways of the dark, sounds she otherwise would not be hearing. So that this is the new, here, in her world. This is the new, yet still dawning.

The draft is not choosy. It is back of the envelope, both sides of the index card, up in the corner of the menu while the waiter forgets your second cup of coffee. It is in the margins, on the end sheets of a book, on manilla, on bond, on onionskin, on loose leaf, in blue books, on newsprint, if you're desperate. Chart paper. Copy paper. Examination table paper. Back of receipts. Blotting paper. Wallpaper.

Maybe, if things were really rough, sandpaper.

Book

In London, the shower stall was cracked, and the mold bloomed into life in the fissures. The wedding we'd traveled for was magistrate, doughnuts, and cigars. The hour the subway closed was the hour we were traveling, me in my high shoes, running, yelling, *Don't let them lock me into an empty tunnel*, while my husband and our young son raced ahead.

Which is all to say that when I returned to our temporary quarters, grumpy and dissatisfied, I was more annoyed than bewildered by the stash of notes that had been shoved beneath the door. Might have even toed a few away with the tip of my constricting shoe before I stooped to pick one up. Then, another.

I was to call people. At once. Regardless of the hour. *Where are you?*

Had I told anyone but my parents, with their famously unlisted phone number, that we'd be in London? Had I told anyone *at all* the name of this leaking hotel? Was there some kind of tracking device I'd not been made aware of? And did they really mean *regardless*?

My agent, my editor, another. The news was in the papers by now—local girl makes good with her debut memoir; local girl is nominated—but it was not my parents who'd been calling. I'd gone from no one to a temporary something, and I'd been absent at my own party. Did I want more than I already had, which was a book in which I try to say *I love you*?

Past midnight in London, I whispered *yes* and *no* and *maybe.*

You will never sell more than three thousand copies of this book, according to the editor who, after saying an emphatic *yes,* sent my pages back to me with a resounding thud. *Every marketing department will reach the same conclusion.*

We don't see this as being a seller, the editor who had bought the book said. *We want it anyway.*

Your words are too literary, and your life is too plain. By one measure or the other, I'd been assigned the role of the would-be writer who wouldn't. There weren't enough stars in the firmament for me to claim one. My small stories in small literary magazines—that was to be my future, if there was to be a future. I was a moonlighter, thieving story and language from the cracks between my actual obligations. Now, I'd been nominated for a prize I couldn't hope to win and still, for two exclamatory nights in my life, I would spend time in the company of the literati. Gerald Stern. Alice McDermott. Harold Bloom.

Who is she? No one. But there I was, suddenly in need of opinions about my words and why I wrote them, suddenly forced to speak of the binaries of a writer's life—the writer versus motherhood, the writer versus time, the writer versus the page—when, in fact, the thought consuming me then was the opposing force of my own mother, whose green eyes burned with irradiated light, who had not called me in London for a reason, who came dressed to the banquet hall on the big awards night in a suit of gold, and who, after John Updike finished his address on the stuff of books and typeface, talked with every editor I introduced her to about her own emerging pages. With the publication of my first book, I was schooled, for I was not to have been the writer in the family; I had, unwittingly, stolen what my mother had wanted for herself. There would be no fixing this, no appeasement. I would perpetually be the cause of my mother's immeasurable sorrow.

She would fly to California, hoping to seduce my agent, a story I would learn from other people. She would not answer my calls if further word on me appeared in the newspaper. She would accuse me of failing her, talk in this way to others about me, and she would never speak to me about the Dard she miraculously located on the shelves of a distant bookstore. What she saw in him. What she wrote of him. If he was mere research or an obsession. For what became forever, my father protected her secrets. I spent ten months packing all the oddments of her home. Dard, somehow, went unnoticed.

Books are hardly zero sum. Books are the life and the life subtracted. In the summoning of words, we lose the hours of our days. We stratify our thinking, seize the glamour of a phrase, assert ourselves through the breathless *don't stop* of semicolons, turn our pages. What a writer never knows is who she'd be without the writing. What sort of wife, what sort of mother, what sort of friend. A writer cannot know whether she'd have been better loved if she'd kept her language to herself. Whether she might have been a better person.

Where does it all begin? What made it possible? The human need to communicate, on the one hand, to tell a story until the story counts. And then, of course, technology. Alberto Manguel, in *A History of Reading*, compresses the technological advance of the book into this sweeping paragraph:

> *Crafting a book, whether the elephantine volumes chained to the lecterns or the dainty booklets made for a child's hand,*

was a long, laborious process. A change that took place in mid-fifteenth century Europe not only reduced the number of working-hours needed to produce a book, but dramatically increased the output of books, altering forever the reader's relationship to what was no longer an exclusive and unique object crafted by the hands of a scribe. The change, of course, was the invention of printing.

Résumé

It's the categorical you: name, experience, education, skills, contact information. That little slice of aspirational poetry: *seeking.* The length of the thing like a child's growth chart—the taller, the longer we grow. The goal is to assert your common decency while propounding your distinctions, to negate the gaps and dissolve the failures. The cracked, broken, smeared do not belong here. Past admonishments and performance plans cannot be trapped between the lines. Remember the rules so that you might live by the rules. Deploy the bold and then the italic. You are standard issue, and you are seamless, and you are likewise special. You will succeed when you finally yield to their interpretations.

What if you were a force of prodigious talents? If you could fresco, carve, and insinuate, if your mind held three dimensions? Would you hoist a sign announcing the superlatives of yourself? Would you graffiti personal ads onto the stones of nearby bridges? Would you paint a portrait of anyone who might whisper, in high places, of your gifts?

In the early 1480s, Leonardo da Vinci was (as he would often be) in need of work. There was a rumored opening with a duke. With competition steep, ingenuity, the story goes, was required, and so the Renaissance man composed a pointed letter, playing up the skills (military, in this case) that he knew the duke was seeking. This narrative résumé separated da Vinci from the crowd. It set a new (and useful) breed of boast into motion. It became one's best possession.

Correspondence

Dear Dard:

He wrote: Might you sell him your "special handmade" paper—750 sheets, maybe 20 × 28 inches? You wrote (it appears that you wrote): There was no such paper for sale at the moment, but when your mill was up to speed, of course.

He wrote: How wonderful to hear that you might be building a mill near Boston, for he was employed as a teacher not too far from your enterprise, and he would love to visit, get a tour. You wrote (it appears that you wrote): Your mill near Boston was facing challenges.

He wrote: He would wait, he would be happy to wait, your paper would be worth it.

Back and forth the letters went, his first arriving on January 24, 1920, his last arriving on November 1, 1925, and what you actually said to Vojtěch Preissig—the Czech typographer, designer, innovator, illustrator, printmaker, children's bookmaker, artisan collaborator, Wentworth Institute teacher—is lost, because your letters to this man are lost, but it is clear that you had affection for him, perhaps because he was a lot like you, with his multiple skills and his paper nerding, with his capacity for making beautiful things. His modesty. His dignity. His waiting, like I said, for his delivery of your paper, which finally, finally, finally arrived, although when it did, in July 1922, it was, indeed, most "excellent" paper, "translucent," even, at its substantial weight, so translucent that the artist's black type and color seeped through, making it impossible to print on both sides.

You stepped up, Dard. You consulted an ink expert. You made certain that your long-awaiting customer would ultimately be pleased, and so your friendship continued, your professional correspondence, until you were engaging in conversations about a school he hoped to build, proposing a Chillicothe visit, imagining a shared print project. The last letter from him to you is capacious with hope. It is capacious with friendship.

You lost touch? I don't know. But having been born in Bohemia and mostly raised a Czech, Preissig chose to return to his country in 1931, where, in the face of Nazi occupation, he became a resistance activist, using his art to combat the occupation forces. He refused to quiet down, to disappear. He refused until, in 1941, he was arrested. Until, on June 11, 1944, in Dachau, he was murdered.

Your friend. Your correspondent. What did you do, Dard, when you learned his fate? What do we do when our friends are gone, when we keep hoping for their letters? Or with the letters that arrive one day and shatter us pristinely? Or when the address we thought we never knew appears in a faded autograph book, far too late for it to save us?

My father loved me, Dard. I found the news last week in an old letter. My mother missed me one long summer; she wrote those words and mailed them. All the letters I wrote that I never sent are falling from my files, talking at me now. I miss the correspondents I lost, the ones I might have treated better.

Almost Letters to Lost Friends

Outlaws

What about you was what about her—you in the white dress your mother made with the angel sleeves and pastel buttons, socks snapped to the knobs of your knees. Your house was two stories of windows, opening. Hers was recumbent with shadows.

Your mother preferred the blonde, Denise. Her house was bright. Her mother was neat. Although it was Denise who taught you to aim a gleaming stream of pee into a seaside bucket placed open end up in her garage while she watched, no gaps in her pearl teeth. The friend you preferred was fashion diffident—leather even in summer, ankle-cuffed jeans, faded Ts, worse, you were encouraged to think, for the darkness that she came from.

You'd cycle past, you'd cycle past, until—from behind the curtain in her forbidden house—you raised her eye, snagged her attention. Was she waiting for you? Did you ask her the question?

She had a banana-seat bike. Your bike was little-girled with handlebar streamers. Getting to the creek was trespass business, the two of you rolling through neighbor yards faster than the cats that chased you. Away from the asphalt. Between clothes hung to dry. Into the trees. Until it was just the two of you and your general disobedience. The slide of tadpoles through your fingers. The confession of birds. The short blue-black rope of the snakes and mica shine, the mesmeric water striders, the cats licking their paws, waiting for the second chase.

Her banana seat taking the lead, her ankles invisible inside their jeans. The wheels of your bikes bumped from neighbors' grass to curb to street, as you followed her down to her house, then cycled back to your house, pedaled up the slanted drive, parked your bike where it belonged, and washed the mud from your fingernails.

After, the sun nearly down, you headed up the hill of that street, turned left at the top, and walked the short distance to the scruff of earth that belonged to no one—an empty, tree-fringed swathe that was open to the stars. You held the lamp of fireflies in punched-lid jars. She might have been there, too. Would she remember?

You can't see those nights, hear her voice, when you remember.

But someone took your picture once, posed the two of you before a camera in honor of fourth grade's end—you in your knee socks, she in her leather. Your father, you're assuming, took that picture. He was never nearly as afraid of that which brought you pleasure.

She moved away first. Or you did.

Either way, you waited for a letter.

Trespass

The house after that was the house your parents sketched on blue graph paper with your father's pencil lead. A house on a mound of earth at a bend in a road with a dark half-moon of trees out back. You were new to that earth, upended, tentative, sloppy postured in purple paisley polyester with perpetually humid hair parted straight above an only slightly better version of your father's nose. You weren't thin anymore, but you didn't know that. You were aloof, thanks to your general loneliness.

She was a pale girl with ginger hair who came by way of trespass—crackling the twigs and rearranging the leaves among the trees you forbade yourself to visit. A bird disturber from up the hill. Your age. Eager.

From the lookout of your room, you watched. Through the trees she came, through the backyard, disappearing then, until you heard her at the front door, knocking. You stayed upstairs until she knocked again and then stayed downstairs, with family near, until she stood and walked into the hall and closed the front door behind her and walked away, down the drive, down the street, up the hill, across the asphalt and concrete.

Of her house, you remember only her room and its amber shade. How she talked music, maybe science. How she showed you the ways she marked her days of blood in a book, calling all those days just one name: Charlie. Side by side on her bed, you sat, as she turned the pages. *There's Charlie.* The blue in her veins.

There's Charlie.

It's easy to see how you hurt her, not easy to know why you did, why you grew impatient with her trespass, her amber room, her Charlie, your own stretch of loneliness, which you improved by finding other friends. Not coming downstairs when she came. Not traveling up the hill and up again, into her amber room. Still not rearranging the leaves in your own forest. Still wearing polyester, the stretch of it that fit you.

It's easy not to forgive yourself, so why should you?

Years later, signing books in a local store, you looked up.

She was standing there.

She had written you a letter.

Avulsion Fracture of the Lateral Malleolus

She's just not that into you, and here you lie, on your back, in your healing room, reckoning the why. This broken ankle in its elephant boot has given you the time.

—

Manhattan was jammed. A president motorcading through town and the subways flooded despite the upbeat version of the sky. You were headed in the same direction for the same reason, and it was her city. What you knew: She'd studied differential equations. She wrote stories. She read signs. She said *This way*, and you followed.

—

You were, to begin with, young writers, mothers, too. Her river was not your river, and there was more room inside her lines for violence, for particularly recalled confession, and your history was minuscule compared to the country she was writing, but still, through the years, you kept each other company—appraising the thermals on Hawk Mountain as if you both had wings and sitting on the warm side of the glass in winter and riding the alphabet of the subterranean tunnels.

Writing your books. Writing your stories.

Once, you stood on the castle rock of Central Park, the pond turtles stacked stone upon stone, and the trees a day away from shucking their own shells, and the tadpoles invisible. The red wing of a blackbird was like a hand that had been dealt.

Afterward, it was Amsterdam to Broadway, Columbus Circle down to the sweet, remembered squalor of Times Square, and on every corner: song. The high hollows of the Peruvians. The mesquite of a jazz trombone. The Mennonites in hairnets and black sneakers.

Listen, you said.

You are almost sure, looking back, that she listened.

Later, you wondered whether you had become the engine of concatenation, two women made radical with unappeasable want, the unassailable desire to remember. You wondered it into a poem. Folded it. Sent it.

The gifts you gave to one another were no larger than a closed hand.

Open it, she'd say.

Open yours.

Sometimes, the phone would ring, and it would be her, and you would drop to the curb and not let the conversation end until the battery barred out.

You read every book she wrote. She read some of yours. Fewer of yours. Then, nothing.

Did you mean to her what she meant to you? Isn't that, always, the question?

—

Still, you did not anticipate how you would not be among the ones she called when she wanted not to be alone, or how you would learn that you no longer fit inside her pantheonic heart, or how you would never again be her first thought or her second, or how when the bone snaps, the bone snaps, leaving shadow between hollows and the strange calcium knitting of you in the improv healing room, writing now these unsent letters.

Dear Bill:

The oldest story being the truest: This love is unfair. Disadvantaged, to begin with, by your beauty, which has only been embellished by the years, glistened and glazed, exaggerated. The white hair the right hair. The square jaw delving into angles.

You have the nonchalant self-confidence of one with nothing needing to be proved, you being good at what you do, you being born that way. How fluid did it feel to be so gifted and so loved, so at home at once with line and color? First-born son, and an artist at that, in a family of coffee trees and war, near assassinations, the thickest possible version of *Don Quixote* passed down to you. Just by being, you are. Just by lifting your charcoal stick to the canvas or page, you assume your ease, you find your quiet, you do not fight for it. Have you ever actually wondered about a fox? Have you ever screamed to outscream the world's noises? Whatever will be will be will come to you, and you shall receive it as it comes, without excessive gratitude.

I worry the meals, I broom the floors, I scrub time for you because time is what you need—in the basement with your clay, in the upstairs room of the converted garage with your easel, charcoal, paint. Most of mostly, I love what you do and what you make, even the old painted lady with the birds in her hair, even the angel dangling from strings, even the ancient man with the stuffed toy and the empty chairs, slanting toward a party. Even you, just you, the parts of you you don't need for yourself, the parts you give away.

You are the artist here. You are the one with theories of color, the rusted Dremel, the tools you anticipate I'll need. You are the one who has always spoken least, because words do get in the way. But when I show you what it is I've made, you do not look away.

Brush for your color. Needle for your thread.

Dear Jeremy:

You would cultivate all the merry colors if you could: raspberry, banana, mango. Sky blue, too, and lime. Your father favors charcoal, green if it's closer to gray, any variety of dark that he can wash and wear without worrying the iron. Not you. Bring the chroma on. Slip your arms through it, your neck, and which is brighter then: Your eyes, or your skin, or your polo? Who taught you to buy Ralph Lauren at the discount mall? Who taught you that raised eyebrow? Who taught you how to buy the smaller size so that your biceps would rise so much more strong, so far more true? Who taught you to shrug casually, why not?

It wasn't me. I know nothing about fashion. I was not born with beauty, as you were, or with your gallimaufry of optimism. You learned to walk while wearing a red jacket. Your tiny running shoes were red-green-blue. You could not be dissuaded from the delight you took in the brightest rising of the moon. You refused to eat from the navy-blue plates because they were, you tried to say, with the language you had then, a most despairing hue.

Go on. *Live.* Put it on. Stride it out. Take color as the sign for what this world is worth and every flower in each garden as your proof, and don't stay home on Friday nights when the girls inside the river bars are wearing celadon and cinnabar, crimson and white silver, and looking so indefatigably good.

And when you stand beside me on the hill above the earth where my mother and now my father lie adjacent in their boxes, when we stand there and above our heads the breeze is the breeze and the bell tower chimes, don't be anyone but you as you tell them, loudly, the stories of you and the you you are becoming. You are the one they want to hear from. You are the one to whom they'll listen, because maybe it's cold down there and goodness warms them, or maybe they've not considered amaranth for a while, or atomic tangerine, or British racing green, and just listening to you through that wood, through that earth, will stipple the thoughts in their dreams.

Dear Dad:

Writing to you from a rented room—morning of rain, fog, and the clouds blowing north. The near tree is woven with birds. Nothing little birds that are not pretty until they fly. Then, they confetti the air. They feather-white it.

There's the window, then a street, then that tree lacing and unlacing its birds, then a river, shallow and beached with stone. Christ wouldn't need a miracle to cross it. He'd just start walking and there He'd be—on the other side, where the last of the leaves on the bones of those trees have gone from green to cinnamon to a simulacrum of sun. Beyond them rises an Appalachian hill, and beyond that, I can't see.

They say there are moose here, bears, wildcats. They say that the abandoned houses on the forest's edge are vaporous—step inside and you'll vanish. The other night, two dogs bisected the head beams of the car my husband was driving. Wolves, I said. Coyotes. But it was dark, and it was late. There is no knowing. There will always be less knowing.

I made so many mistakes, you said, weeks before death took you. I shook my head no. The last test is forgiveness, and through all my years as your daughter, I refused to fail, being stubborn as they come, and then some, and besides, sometimes you loved me. Said you did. Proved it.

I am less complicated without you. Here, in this rented room, watching the fog fool itself into lifting, and the birds making fast white dots, and Christ leaving His footprints on the minor flow of this story. I am less worrying about the end because the end has come. I am less writing the alternative hoping.

You left in the howl of a storm, and it's really something how, in this moment, by this window, the fog and the clouds and the birds are becoming the same soft thing. It's really something that I am here, watching, and you aren't anywhere, except within me. You'd like the birds, Dad. You'd like the river. There is so much more I'd urge to show you.

Dear Mom:

You wore the sweet cream smell of Pond's. Your hair was white around your face and still dark in other places. Your nylons agitated. There was something in your eyes, a small disturbance, but this was my party—my brownies on my table, my friends chinking glasses—and when Bernadette asked whether you were proud of me for the grant I'd won, the room grew quiet. You paused before you said it: *I have another daughter.*

There was a book, my first. You spoke of me behind your hands, your platinum crooked on your wedding-band finger.

There was a book, my second. I wrote your beauty into it, hoping to appease you. But that book also won a grant, so you wouldn't answer the phone, or open the door, or forgive me.

You were always the prettiest one in the room. Your eyes were many colors.

You wanted a book with your name on the cover, but every letter you wrote with your pages attached was returned with the wrong answer.

Ragged with words, I kept writing. I wrote each book because each past book had slipped its frame, because the sentences had gone off in a discord of directions, because the rhythms were evasions of my meaning. I couldn't explain it.

What I had, you did not have. You struggled to stay even. You looked straight through me. You hid the books you bought, for your peculiar reasons.

Although once, Mom, at a restaurant, you reached into your purse and retrieved a check. You paused before you said it: *Because you worked so hard. Your last two mortgage payments.*

Once, you made my son a photo album, handwriting every caption: *Mommy takes such good care of me.*

Once, it was just the two of us, and we were laughing—you snorting the way you did when the thing was really funny.

When you were speaking to me, we spoke daily.

When I went shopping, it was because I loved to buy you presents. Glass apples. Humpty Dumptys. Crisp white bags of Termini Brothers biscotti.

(Leave a package on your doorstep.)

(Hang an angel in your window.)

Dad stole your pages from you and brought them to me. Bill and I did everything we could to try to package them, to sell them, to find an editor, an agent. We failed. You never knew. You told your friends I was to blame for the thing no one could give you.

The night you had the stroke, I was at a cha-cha party, in the margins, watching. A black heat cratered through me, a shot to the heart. I crumpled. Dad called the next day, early. I knew before he told me. I broke every traffic law to reach you, rushed through the hospital halls, broke into your white, strange room. You were losing words fast, words were dying by the second. By the afternoon, there was most of nothing left, but you poking at the air in my direction.

Your last words, Mom, belong to me. Your last words: *I love you.*

We brought you home to die in the glass room. I sat beside you, singing. James Taylor. Rod Stewart. Carly Simon. Billy Joel. Just music, and no books, at last, between us. On your final day, in your final hour, I left you. Drove home through the dark and walked into the night, where the fox and deer smudged the shadows. I felt the knock of something passing, a clean strike against one shoulder. The air was winter. I was running. When I reached the house, I heard the phone. It was Dad. He paused before he said it.

Dear Professor Kephart:

Our time in Kislak came to me when I needed it. After learning about Dard, I returned to my art history project with an equanimity I had not known in a while, and I was ready to take on my final assignment at Penn. I was floored by your studies, the way you are weaving your own story into his, the old books, the way you let me into your process, and the very idea that my professor wanted to show me her personal endeavors.

This is the most touching message I have ever received. I read your words with tears streaming down my face. As this book may be a culmination of your ideas and career, being written into it is a culmination of my time at Penn and an homage to the relationships I have learned to create. And how very apt it is that I am featured in a section that is in part about obsession, my greatest weapon, and my worst demon. I will not forget this. I am astounded. He is so lucky you are the one to tell his story.

And paper. I want to honor this somehow during my year off. I now fantasize about finding myself in a printing shop, stopping for a job with the papermakers, wherever they may be, in Europe, whenever I run out of money. You have me hooked on that one. As you taught me, in a world of chaos, despair, and no ultimate truth, paper binds our stories and makes tangible our constructed meaning.

I will also always cherish your words from another email: "I was coming back to email to say that you, I think, understand being alive, and how to live. Penn didn't teach you that. It is inherent." I shared these words with my mom (unlike the others, I assumed these were not confidential), and she read them aloud during a toast she gave me at a very special graduation celebration.

Ever since your class, my experience of the world has become increasingly interconnected. I see threads. I notice the "binding themes" across my interactions. A scene emerges. I understand how to dance through past and present experiences to make a story come alive. And I nod to the sky and I shake my head in disbelief. I mumble "good one."

You make graduation a little less daunting for me, because I know I have a friend in you, out here in the real world.

With love,

Beatrice

Erasures

Dear Dard:

Didn't he know?

That Edith had died—a sudden death. She'd been standing up. She'd been cleaning. She fell toward her end. You were not at Mountain House but on business in Cambridge. You had already felt slippery inside your own life—nothing much to hope for, nothing much you wished to do—and now you were distraught. *Depressed. Disheartened. Despondent.* Your words. Edith gone.

Didn't he care?

That you'd boarded a plane to London in search of your precipitating past, but that London hadn't saved you? London had changed, your past was gone, your interest in it had vanished, and besides, any story you might hunt down would never be shared with Edith. Edith was not at home, waiting for your letters.

Didn't he see?

That only after Neil M. Clark published a prettily illustrated piece on you in the February 27, 1954, issue of the *Saturday Evening Post*—"Paper Detective," he called it, a happy sobriquet—did you start to lean toward a new sudden preoccupation, something actual and animating to do?

A career that defies classification, Clark writes.

Reading Clark's words, deluged by congratulations, looking back across your life not in London, now, but among your many things at home, you all of a sudden had the audacity to imagine Autobiography Number Two, a follow-up to the book you'd published in 1941, which you'd called *Before Life Began*. Your friends encouraged you. Your heart said, *Do it*. You felt a touch of confidence growing, wondering whether this new autobiography might have big-enough heft and wide-enough appeal to be acquired by a major publisher. Whether it might build your renown, just a little bit. Emancipate a minor psychic lift.

That's when you were put in touch with him—Alfred Knopf. His interest, based on your previous "memoir," was tepid. He wished you were a better writer, he said. He hoped that Autobiography Number Two would include "more sophisticated happenings" than did Autobiography Number One. It was July 1954. Edith had been missing for three years. You needed this. You swallowed hard. You genuflected, did your best. You hoped that Mr. Knopf would find goodness in your (your words) "homely style."

You wrote, wrote more, sent a draft.

Knopf rendered judgment: *Unpublishable.*

Editors can be like that, Dard. I've had my share. They tear you down, or they ignore you. They show you who is boss, they tell you who is better, they point to where you are allowed to sit at their prejudicial table. Editors preen their favorites, and they pound their power, and they allow themselves the final word, the last laugh, too, unless you can forsake it, fool them with a hit, score some reader love, win a prize they didn't recommend you for, but still, on your behalf, to the high and mighty Alfred Knopf, I say: *Have a little heart.*

You swallowed hard. Again. You went back to work. Again. You genuflected. Again. Thanked the big man for his excruciating comments. Flew to Puerto Rico to get some sun and some inspiration, until, three years later, you sent your much-reconsidered seventy thousand words to the mustache man, who acquiesced a *Yes, I'll publish this book*, although he might have deployed a scintilla of enthusiasm.

Then, there was the battle of the titles. You gave Knopf a whopping forty from which to choose. Knopf declared that he liked a whopping none, came up with his own list of sore title losers. *No*, you said, standing your title ground. Thank God. Finally, reluctantly, Knopf agreed to *My Life with Paper*, a title I have (with one adjustment) stolen. Just to show Knopf who's boss. Just to prove whose side I'm on.

Knopf printed four thousand copies of Autobiography Number Two, tipping into each book a piece of original "spirit paper" as well as a sheet of watermarked paper from your Lime Rock mill. The book showed up in stores in the autumn of 1958. It retailed for $5. Your friends were pleased and said you should be pleased as well, but you demurred, worried about minor mistakes, wondered whether you had been too personal (not even a little bit, Dard, not even enough). You consoled yourself that few would read it, just like authors do, because we are so ripe with want and contradiction; we are so twisted. You opened yourself to your own postmortem biographer, Catherine A. Baker, who loves you in her biographer way, whose scholarship is the reason I can relate this part of your story, other parts of your story, and yet (because precision matters in the making of history) is forced to note your inaccuracies, to exclaim them: "But as was true with *Before Life Began*, the veracity of *My Life with Paper* is problematic. Hunter often dated events incorrectly. For example, he stated he first arrived in East Aurora in July 1903—it was 1904. This error appeared in both biographies."

You were writing in the wake of your bereavement, in the thick of your uncertainty, in a life confronting vanish, and I bristle on your behalf. I imagine you reimagining yourself. Chasing the scenes and not the datebooks.

And yet, Dard, books are our freeze-frames. They become, after we are gone, our most implacable selves, and within this book, within all your books, is language that blisters with the blinders of your time, your way of seeing. You brought a Western white man's filter to your travels. You catalogued and named according to your station—smashing the word *primitive* onto Indigenous papermaking, Other-ing your foreign hosts, characterizing some traditions as naïve or ill-informed. Your scholarship was foundational, but all foundations must finally be interrogated, Dard—the implied biases coaxed toward the light and rectified by those such as the translator and publishing consultant Alta L. Price, who are, in her words, "paying more attention to the words we use when we talk about paper, examining how these terms came into circulation and making deliberate changes to the language in order to prevent erasure, remove bias, and lift up all global paper making traditions."

My mother bought your book for $100.

My brother took it from his bookshelf and wrapped it like a present and gave it to me on Thanksgiving Day, which was, in the COVID era, in joint masquerade with Christmas.

I read you, and I wondered about you, and now I turn you into letters, now I write my dissipations.

Death Certificate

We were sat shoulders against shoulders. Our father told us. It was Mischief Night, and tomorrow would be Halloween. Already, the marauders were in the woods by the creek, making trouble. Our mother was in the city, in the place where the dying had been, where my grandmother had lain in the bed in the room on the second floor of the house on the narrow of the street, alone in her dying, those houses crunched like we were sitting, crunched—my brother, my sister, and me. Only my brother's feet touching the floor.

The dress she had been married in hung in the cool cave of her basement, the color of a lamp turned on. Her flea-market paintings stepped one above the next on the stairwell wall. Her blackened pots in the kitchen, and her mirror brush on the dark bureau, and the blues of her music in the shadows.

Mischief Night was getting on. Soon, the trouble would leave the creek and wrap itself into our streets, and I would refuse its coming. I would watch the western sky instead, wait for the whoosh of my grandmother's long dress on the horizon, the soft, unharmed billow of her hair. I had brushed her hair, I had been gentle, she had not been, not always, alone.

Thinking her into the sky.

Learning religion, on the edge of evenfall.

> *Death is an assassin with infinite aliases, and the question of what kills us is tremendously complex. It is also tremendously labile. We ask it with clinical curiosity and keen it in private*

> *grief; we pose it rhetorically and inquire specifically; we address it to everyone from physicians to philosophers to priests. It is as bare as bone and as reverberant as bell metal: Why do we die?*

In "Final Forms: What Death Certifications Can Tell Us, and What They Can't't" Kathryn Schulz traces the history of the death certificate from the early-sixteenth-century device "The Bill of Mortality," to the World Health Organization's eight thousand ways to die enumerated over hundreds of pages in its *International Statistical Classification of Diseases and Related Health Problems,* to the unwieldy number of instruction pages that accompany the single-page death certificate of our times. The "saddest of diplomas," Schulz calls it. "The most mysterious of passports." And, in the end, the ultimate inadequacy and pretense, a summing up that cannot account for so many covert factors.

Death is an assassin with infinite aliases. Consummate words.

My grandmother's cancer was a terrible cancer—greedy and blackening. It was endured with what I understand to have been little to no medical aid. She did not wish to be seen, and she was not seen. She did not wish to be looked at, to be given a verdict, to expose herself to the exploratory hands, and tools, of strangers, to swallow morphine. She spent her final months in the front bedroom of the rowhouse she'd bought on Guyer Avenue in southwest Philadelphia—her name alone on the deed, her silver hairbrush on the dresser, her orange wedding dress in the basement, her hallways shadowed, her legs uncovered when I left the downstairs hush and climbed the stairs to see her.

I knew to leave her room as she covered her legs with the crusted bedsheets. I knew to return. I knew to sit in the dark with her, on the edge of her bed, her hand near my hand, both of us silent. Death coming. Death not yet. Then—?

What is a certificate in the face of grieving?

What is an explanation?

Assassin. Alias. We will all be taken.

Address Book

At the tennis club where we don't belong, there is a restaurant to which she likes to go. Ice in the swan pond and no swans, for it is winter. Willow trees gone gray, attenuated.

Inside: white china, cloth napkins, the slow rhythm of a tennis match going on beyond the pane of glass behind me. It is our Christmas lunch. Just her. Just me. Do not adjudicate the present hour. Take the violet in the green of her eyes. Take her amaranthine beauty and her chary mind and the gift she gives you, wrapped prettily.

It's a Toccata, from Nashville, Tennessee. In the blank parts of the front pages, she has written with blue ink:

> This book belongs to *Beth Kephart from Mom, Christmas Love*
>
> Significant dates to remember: *May 4, Jeff; May 19, Claire; July 19, (the great) Jeremy; August 16, Owen*

My father's birthday, my husband's birthday, my birthday, hers have not been noted. My brother's and my sister's, my nieces' and my nephews' have. All the pages that follow will be mine to demarcate with the names of the friends I wish to keep, the streets where they live, the numbers I might call in the middle of the night. It will be my project, determining whom I wish to keep, and how. The last names first. The house and unit numbers, the names of streets and states (sometimes countries), the zip codes, the phone numbers. Everyone I know, scribbled into one place.

This address book will never leave me. I will fill its empty lines, then ream it out with cards and notes and proof of strange transactions until its binding is busted, and the pages are detaching from their glue, and the white ribbon on the decorative papers has become an ivory color. Most of its people have moved, are gone, have vanished from my life, meaning that the book is mostly questions now, the book is a book about those I've mostly lost. The book says that I will never find them.

Still, I ply it with memory. An email, printed, from the movie man Lee Daniels: *Dreams huh? Please send me your materials.* A list—*fingernails, tight pants, toxic smoke, pink glow*—scratched onto the flip side of a photocopied menu. A typed announcement from my father: *Prudence has dictated that it is time for me to leave our beautiful, memory-filled home of 42 years here in Newtown Square to take up residency in a two-bedroom villa.* A slender printed program announcing the arrival of Jill Lepore, Ph.D., to Villanova University, where, on behalf of a lecture series created in memory of my mother, she will deliver remarks on the life and opinions of Benjamin Franklin's sister. Sticky notes detached from their contracts. A penciled estimate regarding the removal of an ash tree. A hand-lettered thank you from a student: *Good surprises have been uncommon company the last few weeks (months?).* A single dollar bill. The phone number of my son's best friend. Ancient computer passwords. Words from a lost friend, Ivy:

> This is a gift for you from the Palmer Museum of Art at Penn State. I hope you'll like playing with it. It reminded me of you for all sorts of reasons—Latin America, symbols, mystery, poetry, meaning (or the puzzle of it).

If it matters, it is here in the book my mother gave me, when it was just the two of us and no adjudications of that present hour. If I need to know, I return to this source, and all the anguish of all the anguish rinses through me. All the ways I loved my mother incompletely, judged her for the ways she judged me, worked both sides of the negotiation: offensive and defensive.

She had collected Dard by then. He was already in her possession. We didn't speak of him at lunch that day, we didn't talk about her work, for it was secret. If I were to write my mother a letter now and fill it with my questions, I wouldn't know where to send it.

The moment passes. The person, and the places.

But imagine a world without addresses or a world being newly addressed. Deidre Mask does precisely this in *The Address Book: What Street Addresses Reveal About Identity, Race, Wealth, and Power*, writing, "in the eighteenth century, residents protested violently when officials marched through their villages painting numbers on their homes with thick ink made from oil and boiled bones. The people understood the new numbers meant that they could now be found, taxed, policed, and governed, whether they liked it or not. They understood that addressing the world is not a neutral act."

Picture Album

How is it that I moved my father from family house to retirement villa to these two rooms to the earth itself (eighty-four calla lilies pillowing him down, sunflowers lamping his way) and never found his picture album?

The notes in his surprisingly legible twelve-year-old hand: *I have enjoyed Forestry very much and I would like to see a lot of boys take such an educational and interesting course.*

As my share of the refreshments, I brought pine-tree-shaped sugar cookies.

Road song captions written in Number 2 lead. Proof of his dog, Chum, and his father's 1940 Buick, and the twelve ponderosa pine trees he planted about his yard. But who was Sally, this girl beside him in the pictures, with the loose braids and a neatly collared blouse and a skirt cut fashionably, above her knees? She is adolescent feminine in that outpost place where they live.

He never mentioned her, not even when I asked him for his past. He never told me his best stories. He never sat me down and said, *This, too, was me*, and all that time I was saying, *Tell me*. My questions glancing until he had grown too deaf to hear, and after that he was gone, missing.

I take his photographs. I take his captions. I take what I don't know, for my safekeeping.

Here, again, another flea-market find—a rusted metal three-ring binder missing both its covers. The person who didn't want it also did not want to toss it, thought these photographs of abject strangers should find a home elsewhere. It did. It's mine. Because my husband snagged it, and then he didn't want it, and he said, *Here*, and I said, *Okay*. It lives in a drawer with other things I cannot lose. Use?

The photographs are mostly black and white, although, later, there is color. They sit upon tacky gridded paper—some sheets khaki-olive, some sheets black. Along the sides or beneath the bottoms of the first few sheets of photographs are captions written with a crooked blue-ink pen: *Mildred Visher. Alvin Visher. Bancroft School. Melanie and Others Cottage. Boat. Shoreline*. There are pictures of gas stations. Pictures of waist-high balsam wood rockets. Pictures of a young man growing older—his posture not quite straight, his eyes not quite focused, his mouth perpetually twisted around words I cannot hear. When the photographs reveal a small tight room in what might be an institution, I draw my own conclusions, tell myself a story, wonder whether this album persists because no one finally has the right to trash heap another's story.

They happened. It happened. The picture album proves it.

Yielding

Dear Dard:

I failed the room, long and thin as it was, inexpertly heated and further chilled by the winter air that hung fuliginous in the open windows—open for ventilation's sake to the exterior twenty-three degrees.

It was a strait of a room. It was an arcade, a pass-through for those who worked in the floors above and sought the mid-afternoon accommodations of the bathroom just beyond us, the near countdown of microwaved tea, the sudsing of dishes in the proximate sink—all of which was far more emphatic than the talk of the dozen young women I was being paid adjunct wages to teach. Who were double-masked. Who were (some of them) scarved. Who were (some of them) hooded, one or two of them rocking in their chairs with the blue of the cold on the chins that I couldn't see. They were muffled, see? They were losing against the wind in the room, the urban blare, the rinse rush ding flush of the people in the kitchen, their mask one, their mask two, the depleting encumbrance of COVID living.

Through the duck bill of my KN95, I strained to breathe. Through the fog of my progressive-lensed glasses, I struggled to see. Through the viscous cold, I wished to hear the answers to the questions I'd been asking. There, in the soot of the steamed mascara that had left my lashes for the murky underworld of my under-eye shadows. There, in my coat, in my boots, walking student to student and leaning in, listening, discerning, straightening, megaphoning the fraction of the answer I had managed to hear until my own breath gave out and I sputtered, quit.

Everything truncated.

Everything smeared.

Everything dissipating, by which I mean: all those generative teaching years, when I knew how to teach, when teaching, in my own mind, defined me. Yes, I can boast of it now, for it's all left me: I had been good at community. I had been good at trustworthy. I had been good at distributing the right things to read, at prompting the right things to write, at sitting back and long listening, and then sagely suggesting, tacking one idea to a next idea until a student came into possession of her story. I had been good at managing time, which is to say that I'd been good at loving.

Others had been pedagoguing in this room just fine. It was me, and I was failing.

Shorter + shorter, denser + denser, louder + louder, I said, quoting Chang quoting someone. My guppy lips against the mask, my lungs running low on their gas, the ship of my soul going down in the skinny strait of that room in winter, at the end of the second year of COVID, when our battles against the scourge had been all the same and profoundly different.

Mary-Louise Parker and the development of character, I said, rushing my delivery, my words like a stone on a skip across a pond.

Molly McCully Brown and writing haunted, I said. "Bent Body, Lamb," I said. "The temptation is to say that having an identical twin who dies just after birth means living with the hieroglyph of loss carved into you from your earliest breath, but that's imprecise, and a concession to melodrama," I read aloud, from Brown's essay. No traction. No rise in the well-crafted eyebrows of the young women in the room seeking a finer entertainment, a younger, more elastic, more chichi teacher, a COVID-era someone who might more expertly mask breathe, or someone who could chortle at the preposterous circumstances, or, at least, someone whose mascara stayed where it belonged and had not become a metaphor for the fight that she was losing.

Anika Fajardo and alternative histories, I said. "What Didn't Happen," I said, asking the dozen around the miles long and severely anorectic table to write their own versions of Fajardo. I sucked against the KN95 as I read aloud. I gasped. I got to the end—

> I began my life in Spanish. This is true. *Zapato* and *leche* were my first words. I crawled on wooden floorboards and encountered tropical insects as big as soup bowls. I teethed on mango seeds, masticating the sweet yellow flesh until my tiny pearls appeared in pink gums. This is true.

—and then looked up to see how the students who couldn't hear me had been texting, and the student who was bored had been doodling, and the one who had, perhaps, not slept in her own bed the night before had closed her eyes, and, honest to God, I felt so small, I was eternally diminished.

I've never been beautiful, I'm not hip. I'm so unhip that I don't know a more capacitating word for *hip*. But once I was a good teacher, Dard, once I commanded a room like a ship, once I did not drown in my own breath, in the treachery of winter doubt, no coming back from it. The doubt, once it settles in, remains. The lack of becomes a permanent lacking.

What is lost is lost, and every successive comeback is mere tarnish, and we are saved by our own estimations by the kindness of another—a letter, maybe, a story—and so I'm writing this to you because I'm thinking about you, at the end of your life, your body playing tricks. The cortisone they gave you for your condition sometimes blunting your imagination. Your six feet tall carrying 128 pounds weak. Your blind eye still blind, your other eye hurting. Your hale and hearty million miles body; your farming, molding, deckling, couching, cutting, setting, walking body; your crushed into cargo holds, squeezed into railway cars, there among the ox carts body; your hand that ceded to the hand of Gandhi body; your heart that survived the dying of Edith body—that body refused to lift one foot and then the next to climb the tall stairs in your own home by the end of your long living, Dard.

They carried your bed into the Mountain House library and settled you in among books, so that you lived there in your final days, wishing for the sunny south, remembering however you remembered then, until your thoughts grew thin.

You died at 4:30 A.M. Dard II found you. We unbecome. We unbecome. Accept my gratitude for listening.

Obituary (One)

On the morning after the evening that Dolores (Lore) Joan Kephart passed away, the sky was bold and sometimes delicately pink, upward-rising tangerine, spasms of lemon. A sky one only rarely sees in winter.

I had been singing to her, talking. I had left the room of glass in the house where she lived and driven home. I was taking a walk in the dark.

She had gathered around her, in her final days, so many varieties of kindness. She had left behind what we would discover still—a note stuck in a bible, a photograph no one remembered taking, a story she had written, a yellowed newspaper column, an A she had earned on a Russian history paper. On the day of her funeral, a warm breeze blew.

Beauty is the art my mother mastered. On her wide window sills, the orchids bloomed. In her hands, the mashed potatoes whipped, the gravy thickened, the turkey cut tender to the bone, the cake sat properly on its doily. She made the dresses that I wore. She embroidered flowers into collars. Sometimes, we were good to one another. I will be gutted by her letters.

In the weeks since her passing, I have been pondering the many measures of a life—that which dissipates, that which remains. I have been looking up, studying the skies. I have been watching the greening of the stalk of curly willow that sits in a vase in my most sun-filled room. I have considered spring's rumbling things, impatient to rise.

Winter will soon cede to spring. The moon will blaze bright through an afternoon haze. The stars won't leave the sky at dawn. The fox won't run when I, alone in heavy shoes, am walking slowly by.

Obituary (Two)

Horace Leonard (Kep) Kephart—a University of Pennsylvania–trained chemical engineer, a graduate of the MIT Sloan School of Management, a tireless, inventive, and perpetually ethical executive in the oil and specialty-steel industries, and a treasured consultant long into his "official" retirement—passed away on August 4, 2020. He was ninety years old.

He leaves behind three children and their families, who loved him deeply and already miss him beyond their capacity for language. He was preceded in his death by Lore Kephart, his wife of more than fifty years, with whom he built gracious homes, walked beaches in search of dolphins, embarked on memorable adventures, and gathered with friends around unforgettable meals.

Generosity defined Kep Kephart—a largesse of heart, a deep well of gift giving, a philanthropic spirit that was palpably present in his work on behalf of Wills Eye Hospital, Villanova University, Bryn Mawr Presbyterian Church, his family, and others. He was a superb gardener and orchid caretaker. He read fat books on history and politics and thought out loud about what he said mattered. When he moved to W—H— in 2015, his kindness of spirit paved a path toward many new friends with whom he discussed the big and small things in life with energy and sly wit.

In an autobiography he penned in December 2018, Kephart writes, "I consider myself so very lucky." Those of us whose love for him is enduring consider themselves lucky, too.

"The obituary writer said the obituary is the moment when someone becomes history," writes Victoria Chang in *Obit*. Chang's book is built of rectangles—right- and left-justified language tombstones written in commemoration of the death of her father's frontal lobe, her mother's lungs, voicemail, ambition, secrets, hope. *The deaths of.*

Marion Winik's book *The Baltimore Book of the Dead* is built of "mourning songs" and remembrances, humor and invention, a lack of distinction between big lives and small ones because, in the end, there is no distinction, and because, as Winik writes, "Our lives are so full of dead people that any sane way of living involves constant remembrance."

Obit, from the Latin *obitus*, which is to say "to depart, to fall, to go toward, to die." Commemorations of the missing were first inscribed on papyrus newspapers called *Acta Diurna* (Daily Events) in ancient Rome, but paper soon took its historical place as the material conveyance of them. Just brief notices, first, and mostly on behalf of the famous, but the overwhelming human cost of the U.S. Civil War escalated the volume of newsprint remembrances, and the subsequent emergence of new print technologies that no longer relied on the hand-setting of type made further room—in terms of the volume of notices and the number of words deployed in the noticing. From names and dates, to biographies, to stories, the obituary continued to evolve, until, in the aftermath of 9/11, the *New York Times* elevated the form again with "Portraits of Grief: Glimpses of Some of the Victims of the September 11 Attacks":

> *Leon Smith Jr.'s boots just might be impossible to fill. He wore the only size 15's in the Fire Department.*
>
> *With Tommy Knox it was often the little things. The way he put toothpaste on his wife's toothbrush when he got up before her, almost every day.*

More than anything else, Mohammad Salman Hamdani wanted people to see him for who he truly was, not for who he seemed to be.

Just 10 minutes before the first plane struck the World Trade Center, Valerie Joan Hanna called Glenn Hughes, her husband of 29 years, to remind him "to take care of the animals," he recalls. That would be Ramses the goat, Quito the llama and the flock of assorted ducks, chickens and turkeys they had been assembling on their 23-acre farm in Dryden, N.Y., near Ithaca.

"The fox won't run," I wrote of my mother. "Superb gardener and orchid caretaker," I wrote, of my father. Wanting more space, as I wrote, which is to say wanting more time, which is to ask: What do we actually ask of an obituary, beyond the purpose that their writing gives to days that lose their shape to sorrow?

After Life

Dear Dard:

On a frontispiece or above a caption, in the pages of one of your books that was made with your own paper. Above the crease in a newspaper. In the shine of the *Saturday Evening Post*. In the book your son and grandson made.

> Father diligently at work cleaning bricks from the iron foundry in 1929. These old bricks were used in rebuilding the brick end and chimney of the mill. Almost each brick was chosen for color balance during the process of laying them, displaying Father's concern for detail.
>
> Dard Hunter examines a proof from "Old Papermaking" at his press.
>
> Dard Hunter demonstrating the various processes of making paper by hand at M.I.T. to a special group from the Twelfth American Philatelic Congress who met in Boston, Massachusetts, November 15, 16, 17, 1946.

Portraits. You.

I lean in close, desperate to see. I activate the immotile with my imagination. So that you speak or maybe hum. So that you turn the white carnation in the lapel of your suit jacket with fingers worn from making. So that you regale the boy and his teddy bear who sit by feet—your first son, who would grow up with your name and in your image.

All those miles, all that hoisting, all that standing patiently in place over type and ink and wet watermarked paper in damp or hot or poorly heated places have not lessened you. Your height is undiminished, but you don't exert it, don't press it to your advantage over others. You like a good suit, a vest, a tie, or you like your shirtsleeves rolled in the southeast Asian sun, or you tuck your knickers into your tall socks, but you are never underdressed, Dard, not for any photographed occasion. Your bright hair silvers with the years, yet the tidal waves remain; you push them back from your broad forehead.

There is so much room, Dard, in your face. There is so much *here.* There is so much *let me show you.* There is so much that remains.

Envelope

The poets fall to their knees—the long shelf where they'd been
perched quivering, then slipping, until Williams Kooser Pastan
Wright Milosz Kunitz Glück Hirshfield Stern Oliver Rich Forché
are sent slumping and plunging, knocking their heads on their way
to the floor, scuffing the stuff of their spines. I run through the
furze of morning sun to break the cascade, but they fall, the poets
sprawl. Bleached shells fall with them. Photographs. The dust of
a hummingbird's nest. A silver spoon. The signature of Rosanne
Cash. Everything, in an instant, is declassified, and this is how we
find the parts of us we've lost: in the things that fall in the room
we now must rearrange—not just the shelves and the shells and the
poets, but the antique spinning wheel and the green glass hippo and
the stuff in the bruised plastic bins that must now be replaced.

Slide the poets to one side, the shells, the spoon, and sit. Snap the
lids on the bins and lift, and a soft plume blows, the aromatics of
old paper. The letters, homework, cards, reports, the words in pencil
and in paint, the three-hole-punched, the ribboned. Gentle now, for
this paper breaks, its glucose chains are strained, there is the short-
fibered havoc of time's disarray:

> Oh Oh laughed Sally. See that animal with two tails . . . I
> like Spring because it brings back all the birds and they will
> eat with us again . . . In my city the buildings will look like
> the things they produce . . . The Titanic was a 1912 disaster.
> It carried a hope and an era, of class, style, and snobs . . .
> Like a ballerina, you lift your pure white skirts to the sky
> and curtsy to the blowing orchestra of grass . . . Please excuse

> ____from all classes after 6th period on Tuesday, March 28th. We have a Hi Q meet . . . It gives me great pleasure to inform you of your admission . . . It has been so long since our last contact, I'm not sure where . . . Evaluation of part-time employee Beth Kephart . . . The Trustees of the University of Pennsylvania request the honor of your presence at the Two Hundred and Twenty-Sixth Public Commencement . . .

It is days before I find my father in the tired envelopes that have lain dormant, for decades, in one bin. I pull his letters through torn edges, and I am twenty-two again—alone in the house up north while the family spends the summer in a Spanish-moss beach town. I am carrying injustice forward, refusing to forgive my mother for loving me less, or so her words have made it seem, the way she looks at me, or doesn't, the way she watches me not eat, the way she practices her secrets, what is hers, what is hers to keep. My battle plan is a lonesome independence, a clerical job among ancient, bright-toothed dentists in a murky university basement. Every friend I have lives somewhere else. The city is smog. My father keeps me company with nonsense:

> It's now about 10 o'clock on what promises to be a hot, sunny Saturday. It will be a race between 5 MPH bike riding, walking to the beach or just sitting on the deck today; we have to conserve our energy because we are going to the Playhouse tonight on the last evening of its smash hit production of *My Fair Lady*.

My father worries:

> Incidentally, if you don't want to have a completely prostrate mother on your hands—GET YOUR WEIGHT BACK UP 10–15 POUNDS AND QUIT WALKING ON SOME OF THE BACK ALLEYS OF PHILADELPHIA. As a suggestion, you could always get

> some shrimp or fish from the Seafood Connection in Bryn Mawr—they also have some very delicious vegetables and fruit. Try eating some small bowls of cereal with a little milk. EAT POTATOES—some fresh orange juice BREAD. Eat Out Once In A While With Friends. Betsy, it's very easy when living alone to cheat yourself out of eating. Please don't!
>
> Remember, the paragraph above was not Fatherly Advice—it was a PLEA.

My father writes as if I'm there with him, learning laziness:

> It's a somewhat grey dripping morning which seems to be having difficulty deciding what kind of day it wants to be. It is ideal for legitimizing the feeling of laziness which has dominated my body these last couple days. I must either succumb to it and enjoy it without thinking about what I could be doing or just snap out of it and "get with it." [This is such a major decision that maybe I'll procrastinate a little longer.]
>
> I've overexercised my writing muscles and must go lie down and rest. Have fun. We love you very much.
>
> Love,

My father waits:

> Please try to pin down one or two options on when you might break away and join us here.

What I was to him, what he was to me—in the folds of the paper inside the torn envelopes, in the summer when I taught myself the habits of resistance and hardened myself to his entreaties. The way I relinquished the version of me that might have been me, so that later I could not get back to this, to the father who loved so easily, who still believed that with the right found words, he would finally persuade me: *Come back. Trust.*

It's not that old paper changes the past. It's that it dislocates long prejudice, shifts the landscape of our seeing. It returns the man at the edge of the sea who is watching the waves for dolphin sheen without us, riding his bike beneath the heavy moss without us, buying two doughnuts and eating them both, because we're not there to share them, because staying away, because famishing ourselves, has become our radical rebellion.

Dear Beth Ellen, Dear Beth, Dear Betsy, Dear Daughter, Dear Friend, Dear Traveller [??]—

The cellulose cracks. The dust plumes. Memory is aromatic, and we cannot change who we didn't become, but we can rearrange our love, depose the facts that were, retrieve from the bin the one last envelope, tall and wide and graying, marked with a man's engineering hand: BETH & BILL WEDDING. Records & General Info. June 28, 1985. We can see that all of what he planned is here, everything he paid for. The discount wedding dress and the preposterous hat. The stretch limousine from Ralph R. D'Abruzzo. The four-tiered wedding cake, no rosettes. The flowers from Albrecht's. The Third Stream Band, the food and champagne and open bar for the guests he listed on successive graph-paper sheets, one after the other, these names of people he mostly did not know, including the family of the man the oldest daughter was to marry, he had to trust this daughter, the one who had not watched the sea with him when he had asked so nicely. Lists of photographs, lists of gifts, lists of lists, a page carrying this header: *Where to change from Wedding Dress and Tuxedo, what to wear, how to get to first night place,*

. . . *the first night place*, and now, in a crumple, nearly overlooked, is a folded index card, and on the card are the words he wrote to bless this daughter's marriage. Words he must have written and practiced and slipped into a pocket on that rainy wedding day, the hard seam of the folded card the weight he carried, the words becoming words he gave and then thought to save so that his daughter might find them when she'd come to miss him most, all these decades on:

> Dear God, we are so very blessed by your gifts of love, family & friends, and May we never lose sight of how precious—how fragile—these gifts are . . . Help Beth and Bill weather the storms of life.

The daughter cannot break the tilt, the fall, in her furze of sun. She cannot stop the sprawl. She is the one now on her knees, and now she stands, she leaves the house, her vision blurred. She buys her father bundled sunflowers. She drives. She parks. She drapes the flowers, one by one, across the arc of his granite stone. She studies his name in the marker and her mother's name beside his, and she will, she knows, rescue her mother's words soon, she will retrieve them from the ragged envelopes. The deer will visit her parents when she's gone. The birds above will caw.

Envelope (*The New Shorter Oxford*): 1) A wrapper, a covering; an enveloping layer or structure. 2) The covering of a letter, now a piece of paper folded to form a packet, usu. with a flap that can be sealed, for completely enclosing a document, etc.

Subtract the final *e*, and it is everything, surrounding and touching on all sides.

Will

The fall, the stubble, the anther. Of the iris I stole from the rhizomatic bed and the scissoring green of the leaves. To press into permanence, I think. Tucking the harvest between two thin, white paper sheets.

Now comes a half-inch board, now two twelve-pound weights.

Time.

I leave the makeshift flower press to its airless squeeze. Still leave it. Return to it weeks later and remove the weights, remove the board. Peel back the first thin white sheet of paper.

The apportioned iris has slipped its fate, shed its skin. Only a ragged tattoo of color remains, seeped into the second sheet of paper. Like a flower painting itself, or imagining its own shadow.

It is all yours now. Do what you will.

Epilogue

Dear Dard:

You left them exhilarated.

You left them bewildered.

You left them chasing.

They'd find your books in libraries, your artifacts in museums, your articles in the crinkle of old newspapers, and turn, but you were not there to answer questions. They'd arrange for their own paper odysseys and return, telling stories of the journeys. They'd give their ingenuity and hours to the making of handmade paper—in an Indiana barn; in a SoHo loft; in a Riverhead, Long Island, basement—and to beguiling children and grown-ups with machines that "hand"made paper, and to making art of handmade paper, and to writing their own books on paper, and to teaching would-be scholars paper, and to interviewing the papermakers, and to interrogating the language of paper, interrogating *your* language, Dard. They'd drive the hill to your house in Chillicothe, and walk beneath the noble tree, and enter the house where you once lived, so that they might sit in the shadow of your yearning. Museums, societies, institutes, conferences, magazines, newsletters, clubs—it's all semicolons and parentheses, this afterlife of the life you lived with paper.

If I have done anything spectacular.

My mother died before I knew she knew you—your book on her shelf, the bookseller's receipt lodged in your pages. On no paper that I've found is there the story of that story—how she came toward you, what she sought within you, what she made of your obsession, whether she sympathized or whether she judged you, whether, because of you, she traced her life through paper. Paper, like memory, is fiber, fragile, fungible, mortal, succumbing to the elements and time. Paper, like memory, confirms or shocks or whispers, but only when we find it.

You don't know me, Dard. You'll never know me. But you have brought me here, to the end of this chase, through the ephemera of paper. I am what I have found in the files, boxes, bags. I am also every page that slipped away, will be forever missing.

Acknowledgments

The list is long, the gratitude eternal.

Alyson Hagy, in the midst of your busy season: I sent you words about a magic show, and you said: *Beth, keep going.* Debbie Levy: I said *doilies*, and you said *doilies*, and it was the sound of the sigh in you that made me want to do my best for all those who favor paper. Katrina Kenison, I effused, and you encouraged. Sara Beth West, your questions make every quest a more-meaningful endeavor. Robin Black, you leaned toward me in the lobby of a city hotel and listened as I imagined this book into emergence. Abigail Thomas: I couldn't get the hardest part right, and you knew that I was struggling, and so you opened your door, and I sat in that chair, and while Sadie lay there at my feet, you asked the perfect questions.

The wildly beautiful memoirists of the University of Pennsylvania: You sat in your chairs around our long table, and I hunkered down beside you—in awe of your work and your convictions, tested by your questions, privileged by your necessary friendships. Beatrice Karp: You, too, said yes, and there we were, and here, in these pages, are the words you wrote that saved me—I am so very grateful. Lynne Farrington and John Pollack, you welcomed me into your Kislak, generated roadmaps, offered sympathy, celebrated the size and heft of the Dard Hunter books you brought to me from your archival shelves, turned the making of this book into a vibrant joy. Christine Nelson: You changed the shape of the diary for me. Timothy Barrett: You honored me with the probing nature of our conversation. Susan Gosin: You remembered so vividly that I came to feel that I was there, at the invention of your paper. Alta L. Price and Radha Pandey: You opened your hearts and helped me see more than I could have seen on my own. Virginia Howell, Robert C. Williams Museum of Papermaking director: You preserve the legacy, shape the future, and share the artifacts and the stories that I had been chasing; thank you for your hospitality and breadth of knowledge and insight.

Shaun Vigil: You shared my wild enthusiasms, you believed we could make something. Will Forrest: You helped make sure that I got it right. Heather Wilcox, you read with reassuring care. Kate Nichols, you made beauty. Gary Kramer, few are better at what you do than you are. To everyone else at Temple University Press, an admiring thank you.

Dard Hunter III: This book is proof of the magnanimity of your own imagination, your expert driving directions, your hospitality, and, even if *taciturn* sits high on your list of favorite words, your gift for storytelling.

The editors who published pieces of this book, or lines from this book, often in very different forms, in their beloved magazines, with these original titles: *Autofocus* ("Unvanishing"), *Blood + Bourbon* ("Featherwhite"), *Brevity* ("The Memoirist's Dilemma"), *The Curator* ("Moving the Type" and "Photograph of a Lost Oil Painting"), *Lines and Stars* ("Stitchwork"), *Phi Kappa Phi Forum Magazine* ("Family Tree"), *The Raven's Perch* ("Spreadsheeting the Void"), *Tiny Spoon* ("Overjoy Cruise"), and *Upstreet* ("The Sum of Which Parts").

Jeff, this book was launched by way of a Christmas gift given at Thanksgiving: *Here*, you said, and so it began. Bill: You have taken my obsessions on as your own—ordering deckles and molds, blending carrageenan and stirring alum, assuming the directorship of shipping, making every day the only adventure I will ever need. Jeremy: You bless me every single day with your faith in me. Mom and Dad: You teach me still about our past and how I'm meant to love.

Sources

Books by Dard Hunter (Consulted for This Book)

Hunter, Dard. 1923. *Old Papermaking*. Chillicothe: Mountain House Press.

———. 1927. *Primitive Papermaking*. Chillicothe: Mountain House Press.

———. 1930. *Papermaking through Eighteen Centuries*. New York: William Edwin Rudge.

———. 1936. *Papermaking in Southern Siam*. Chillicothe: Mountain House Press.

———. 1939. *Papermaking by Hand in India*. New York: Pension Printers.

———. 1943. *Papermaking: The History and Technique of an Ancient Craft*. New York: Knopf.

———. 1947. *Papermaking in Indo-China*. Chillicothe: Mountain House Press.

———. 1950. *Papermaking by Hand in America*. Chillicothe: Mountain House Press.

———. 1958. *My Life with Paper: An Autobiography*. New York: Knopf.

———. 1978. *Papermaking: The History and Technique of an Ancient Craft*. New York: Dover Publications Edition.

Articles by Dard Hunter (Consulted for This Book)

Hunter, Dard. 1938. "Scenes from an India in Ferment: Gandhi Visited." *New York Times*, May 15.

———. 1943. "Ancient Chinese Invention Held Vital Today—It's Paper." *Los Angeles Times*, March 7.

Books and Articles about Dard Hunter (Consulted for This Book)

Adler, Elmer. 1925. "Four Centuries of Papermaking: Dard Hunter as Author, Publisher, Typemaker and Printer." *New York Times*, April 16.

Baker, Cathleen A. 2000. *By His Own Labor: The Biography of Dard Hunter*. New Castle, DE: Oak Knoll Press.

Clark, Neil M. 1954. "Paper Detective." *Saturday Evening Post*, February 27.

Coleman, Brian D. 2022. "The Historic Home of Dard Hunter." *Old House Journal*, January 5.

"Dard Hunter, 82, an Authority on Paper and Printing, Is Dead: Scholar Analyzed Japanese Paper during Wartime, Published Own Books." 1966. *New York Times*, February 22.

Duffus, R. L. 1936. "A Paper Trail through the Far East." *New York Times*, September 6.

———. 1939. "Dard Hunter on Papermaking by Hand in India." *New York Times*, June 25.

"Expert Ready to Sail on New Paper Search: Dard Hunter Leaving Tomorrow for India to Get Data and Actual Pages of a New Book." 1937. *New York Times*, October 8.

Hunter, Dard, II, and Dard Hunter III. 1998. *Dard Hunter and Son, with a Foreword and Notes by Henry Morris*. Newtown, PA: Bird and Bull Press.

Kegler, Richard, and Timothy Conroy, eds. 2000. *Dear Mr. Hunter: The Letters of Vojtěch Preissig to Dard Hunter, 1920–1925*. Rochester, NY: P22 Editions.

Winterich, John T. 1958. "Pages That Tell a Story." *New York Times*, November 9.

Books, Magazines, and Articles on Paper and Papermaking:

Barrett, Timothy. 2005. *Japanese Papermaking: Traditions, Tools, and Techniques*. Warren, CT: Floating World Editions.

Basbanes, Nicholas. 2013. *On Paper: The Everything of Its Two-Thousand-Year History*. New York: Vintage Books.

Green, James. 1990. *The Rittenhouse Mill and the Beginnings of Papermaking in America*. Philadelphia: Library Company of Philadelphia.

Heller, Jules. 1978. *Papermaking*. New York: Watson-Guptill Publications.

Hiebert, Helen, and Michael G. LaFosse. 2022. *The Art of Papercraft: Unique One-Sheet Projects Using Weaving, Quilling, Pop-Up, and Other Inventive Techniques*. North Adams, MA: Storey Publications.

Kuransky, Mark. 2016. *Paper: Paging through History*. New York: Norton.

LaFerla, Jane, and Veronica Alice Gunter, eds. 2004. *The Penland Book of Handmade Books: Master Classes in Bookmaking Techniques*. New York: Lark Books.

Pandey, Radha, and Aisha Wahab. 2022. "Terminology and Language: A Conversation." *Hand Papermaking* 37 (1): 8.

Price, Alta L. "Rice, Rice, Baby: What We Talk about When We Talk about Paper." *Hand Papermaking* 37 (1): 3.

Studley, Vance. 1977. *The Art and Craft of Handmade Paper*. New York: Dover Publications.

Toale, Bernard. 1983. *The Art of Papermaking*. Worcester, MA: Davis Publications.

Source Material for Legends Not Otherwise Cited in the Text:

Baby Book:

Golden, Janet, and Lynn Weiner. 2011. "Reading Baby Books: Medicine, Marketing, Money and the Lives of American Infants." *Journal of Social History* 44 (3): 667–687.

Scrapbook:

Ott, Katherine, Susan Tucker, and Patricia P. Buckler. 2006. *The Scrapbook in American Life*. Philadelphia: Temple University Press.

Menu:

Whitaker, Jan. 2018. "Children's Menus." *Restaurant-ing through History*, April 22. https://restaurant-ingthroughhistory.com/2018/04/22/childrens-menus/.

Diary:

Thomas, Abigail. 2008. *Thinking about Memoir*. New York: Sterling. Used with permission from Abigail Thomas.

Amateur Art:

"About Us." The Froebel Trust. https://www.froebel.org.uk/about-us.

Irving, Joan. 1997. "Construction Paper: A Brief History of Importance." *The Book and Paper Group Annual*, vol. 16. The American Institute for Conservation. https://cool.culturalheritage.org/coolaic/sg/bpg/annual/v16/bp16-07.html.

Oatmeal Box:

"Global Challenges." n.d. *The World Counts*. https://www.theworldcounts.com /challenges/consumption/other-products/environmental-impact-of-paper.

Recipe:

Nicosia, Marissa. 2022. "Cooking in the Archives." *Rare Cooking*, May 4. https://rarecooking.com/2022/05/04/to-make-a-leach-of-dates/.

Wall, Wendy. 2016. *Recipes for Thought: Knowledge and Taste in the Early Modern English Kitchen*. Philadelphia: University of Pennsylvania Press.

Paper Game:

Shefrin, Jill. 1999. *Neatly Dissected for the Instruction of Young Ladies and Gentlemen in the Knowledge of Geography: John Spilsbury and Early Dissected Puzzles*. Toronto: Cotsen Occasional Press, Cotsen Family Foundation, Coach House Printing.

Turchi, Peter. 2014. *A Muse and a Maze: Writing as Puzzle, Mystery, and Magic*. San Antonio: Trinity University Press.

Sewing Pattern:

Campbell, Douglas S. 1989. *Dictionary of Literary Biography*. Farmington Hills: Gale.

Emery, Joy Spanabel. 2020. *A History of the Paper Pattern Industry: The Home Dressmaking Fashion Revolution*. New York: Bloomsbury Academic.

Ross, Ishbel. 1963. *Crusades and Crinolines: The Life and Times of Ellen Curtis Demorest and William Jennings Demorest*. New York: Harper and Row.

Whitley, Lauren. 2005. *Encyclopedia of Clothing and Fashion*. Farmington Hills, MI: Scribner.

Sheet Music:

Bewley, John. "Alexander Reinagle." Penn Library, Keffer Collection of Sheet Music.

Hopkinson, Francis, and James Wisen. 1788. "Account of the Grand Federal Procession, Philadelphia, July 4, 1788. To Which We Added, Mr. Wilson's Oration, and a Letter on the Subject of the Procession." Philadelphia: M. Carey.

"A Soundtrack to History: Early American Sheet Music from the Library of Congress." 2018. *Music Educators Journal* 104 (8): 15–16. Published by Sage Publications, Inc., on Behalf of MENC, the National Association for Music Education.

Blueprints:

Case, Stephen. 2015. "'Land-marks of the Universe': John Herschel against the Background of Positional Astronomy." *Annals of Science* 72 (4): 417–434.

Dolkart, Andrew S. 2005. "Waldorf-Astoria." *Journal of Decorative and Propaganda Arts* 25:31.

How to Read Blueprints. 1926. Philadelphia: David McKay.

Keats, Jonathan. 2009. "The Blueprint: A Failure for Photography, It Was Long Irreplaceable for Duplicating House Plans." *Scientific American*, September 1.

Rare Books:

Bodmer, George. 1998. "A. S. W. Rosenbach: Dealer and Collector." *The Lion and the Unicorn* 22 (3): 277–288. doi:10.1353/uni.1998.0032.

Cournos, John. 1937. "The Thrills of a Book Collector: Dr. Rosenbach Feels That Hunting Rare Books Offers More Stirring Adventures Than Trapping Wild Animals in the Jungle." *New York Times*, January 3.

Rosenbach, A. S. W. 1927. *Books and Bidders*. Boston: Little, Brown.

———. 1936. *A Book Hunter's Holiday: Adventures with Books and Manuscripts*. Boston: Houghton Mifflin.

Starrett, Vincent. 1952. "Books Alive." *Chicago Daily Tribune*, July 27.

Dard Hunter Letter on Possession:

Museum captions courtesy of the permissions granted by the Robert C. Williams Museum of Papermaking at Georgia Tech.

Ticket:

Tickets sourced from the Civil War Broadsides collection of the Library Company of Philadelphia. Used with permission of the Library Company of Philadelphia.

Library Card:

City Hall Branch. Photographic Prints. Philadelphia: Free Library of Philadelphia. https://libwww.freelibrary.org/digital/item/44655.

Receipt:

Library Company of Philadelphia, Ephemera Collection, Receipts 3321.F .52, https://digital.librarycompany.org/islandora/object/digitool%3A120035. Used with permission of the Library Company of Philadelphia.

Legal Tender:

Senchyne, Jonathan. 2017. "Rags Make Paper, Paper Makes Money: Material Texts and Metaphors of Capital." *Technology and Culture* 58 (2): 545–555.

Smithsonian Office of Educational Technology. 2016. "Smithsonian Learning Lab Collection: Revolutionary Money." *Smithsonian Learning Lab*, August 10. https://learninglab.si.edu/collections/revolutionary-money/5bPtu494NLUNxTk6.

File Folder:

Robertson, Craig. 2019. "Granular Certainty, the Vertical Filing Cabinet, and the Transformation of Files." *Administory* 4 (1): 71–86. https://doi.org/10.2478/adhi-2019-0005. Licensed under CC BY-NC-ND 4.0. https://creativecommons.org/licenses/by-sa/4.0/legalcode.

Ballot:

Cheng, Alicia Yin. 2020. *This Is What Democracy Looked Like: A Visual History of the Printed Ballot.* Princeton, NJ: Princeton Architectural Press.

Lepore, Jill. 2008. "Rock, Paper, Scissors: How We Used to Vote." *The New Yorker*, October 13.

Luminary:

"Luminary." 2017. *Online Etymology Dictionary*, April 29. https://www.etymonline.com/word/luminary.

Ortega, Pedro Ribera. 1973. *Christmas in Old Santa Fe.* Santa Fe, NM: Sunstone Press.

Report Card:

Schneider, Jack, and Ethan Hutt. 2014. "Making the Grade: A History of the A–F Marking Scheme." *Journal of Curriculum Studies* 46 (2): 201–224.

Spreadsheet:

Coate, C. J., and M. C. Mitschow. 2018. "Luca Pacioli and the Role of Accounting and Business: Early Lessons in Social Responsibility." In *Research on Professional Responsibility and Ethics in Accounting*, vol. 21, edited by C. Jefrey, 1–16. Bingley, UK: Emerald Publishing. https://doi.org/10.1108/S1574-076520180000021001.

Fischer, Michael J. 2000. "Luca Pacioli on Business Profits." *Journal of Business Ethics* 25 (155.4): 299–312.

Sangster, Alan. 2021. "The Life and Works of Luca Pacioli (1446/7–1517)." *Humanist Education* 57 (1): 126–152.

Dard Hunter Letter on Making:

Frame, Richard. 2006 [1692]. "A Short Description of Pennsilvania." National Humanities Center. http://nationalhumanitiescenter.org/pds/amerbegin/permanence/text4/FramePennsylvania.pdf.

Broadsides:

Rosenbach, A. S. W. 1929. "Extra! Extra!" In *A Book Hunter's Holiday: Adventures with Books and Manuscripts*. Houghton Mifflin.

Pulp:

Hunter, Dard. 1930. *Papermaking through Eighteen Centuries*. New York: William Edwin Rudge.

Postcard:

"History of Postcarding." 2020. *World Postcard Day*. https://worldpostcardday.com/history.

Toal, Bob. 2020. "The Lipman Postal Card." *Postcard History*, November 1. https://postcardhistory.net/2020/11/the-lipman-postal-card/.

Certificate:

Brown, Leslie, ed. 1993. *The New Shorter Oxford: English Dictionary, Thumb Index Ed.* Oxford, UK: Clarendon Press.

Gift Wrap:

B., Samantha. 2017. "Ask the Hallmark Historian: Stories from Our Gift Wrap History." *Think. Make. Share*, December 27. https://www.thinkmakeshareblog.com/gift-wrap-history/.

Spencer, Laura. 2017. "100 Years Ago, Holiday Presents Didn't Always Look Great, but Kansas City's Hallmark Fixed That." *KCUR*, December 15. https://www.kcur.org/arts-life/2017-12-15/100-years-ago-holiday-presents-didnt-always-look-great-but-kansas-citys-hallmark-fixed-that.

Wagner, Ruth. 1960. "Takes Wraps Off Wrapping." *Washington Post and Times Herald*, June 12.

Prescription:

"The Negro in Pharmacy: Negro Colleges of Pharmacy New York." 1897. *Druggists' Circular and Chemical Gazette (1866–1906)*, November 1.

Résumé:

Findlen, Paula, and David Carrier. 2014. "Seeking a Job, Renaissance Style." *Leonardo* 47 (5): 529–531. https://muse.jhu.edu/article/555707.

Death Certificate:

Schulz, Kathryn. 2014. "Final Forms." *The New Yorker*, March 31.

Obituary (Two):

Chen, David W., Anthony DePalma, Jan Hoffman, Lynette Holloway, Nat Ives, Tina Kelley, Patrick McGeehan, Michelle O'Donnell, and Lydia Polgreen.

n.d. "Portraits of Grief: Glimpses of Some of the Victims of the September 11 Attacks." *New York Times*. https://archive.nytimes.com/www.nytimes.com/pages/national/portraits/?p=041.

Envelope:

Brown, Leslie, ed. 1993. *The New Shorter Oxford: English Dictionary, Thumb Index Ed.* Oxford, UK: Clarendon Press.

Beth Kephart is a teacher of memoir, the co-founder of Juncture Workshops, and a book artist. She is the award-winning author of more than three dozen books in multiple genres, including *Wife | Daughter | Self: A Memoir in Essays* and *We Are the Words: The Memoir Master Class*. Her book *Flow: The Life and Times of Philadelphia's Schuylkill River* (Temple) has become a regional classic. Visit her online at bethkephartbooks.com and bind-arts.com.